FQ

FREQUENCY
INTELLIGENCE™

REY ABADI

FQ
Frequency Intelligence™

For permission requests, contact: Purpose Publishing via email at
contactus@purposepublishing.com.

For speaking engagements, interviews, bulk orders, or
promotions contact the author and stay connected at
www.FrequencyIntelligence.com

Printed in the United States of America

Paperback ISBN - 978-1-965319-55-0
eBook ISBN- 978-1-965319-56-7

Purpose Publishing LLC.
13194 US Highway 301 South, Suite 417
Riverview, Florida 33578

www.PurposePublishing.com

FQ–Frequency Intelligence™

The Future of Inner Intelligence

First, there was IQ. Then EQ.
Now, FQ: The Next Human Intelligence

FREQUENCY Intelligence Methodology
The New Era of Energy Intelligence

Frequency Intelligence is a revolutionary personal growth system that combines astrology, numerology, biorhythms, and real-time energy tracking with artificial intelligence. The purpose is to help users optimize their lives by aligning with their natural energy cycles and cosmic blueprint.

This system is not just predictive—it's prescriptive. It offers daily guidance, intuitive tools, and AI-powered support that adapts to each person's unique frequency pattern.

by Rey Abadi

Table Of Contents

Introduction
The Signal Before the Breakdown

There are moments in life when the world as we know it shifts—subtly at first, then all at once. One day, you wake up and realize the story you've been living is too small. A quiet whisper says, *There's more. You came here to create something bigger.*

This book was born from one of those moments.

I didn't set out to build an AI system. I didn't set out to merge artificial intelligence with ancient metaphysical wisdom. I set out to make myself happy. To find freedom.

For years, I pursued what many would call success. I founded a sustainable luxury shoe brand rooted in long-term values. I was a strategist, a consultant, a creative, a founder. I spent over a decade helping organizations grow, guiding leaders toward more conscious choices. On paper, it all looked right—beautiful, meaningful, profitable.

Yet underneath, I felt deeply out of sync. I wasn't burned out in the traditional sense—I was misaligned. My energy, creativity, and intuition were being channeled into systems that didn't speak the language of my soul. I had spent years following models of leadership and productivity that never felt like home. I was solving the wrong problems while using someone else's playbook.

I followed the rules. I built with integrity. I chased the ideal of what success should look like, but I was soul-tired. Drained by a world that didn't recognize the intelligence I was wired to follow.

A Quiet Knowing

I've always been a seeker—a strategist of invisible systems. Even in my earliest work—from writing my thesis on the green movement to designing shoes with soul—I was chasing something more fulfilling: How do we create in alignment with what truly matters? In 2025, something shifted. Quietly, then unmistakably. A download. A vision. A call.

It didn't come from logic. It came from the place where inner resonance speaks louder than reason. A space I had trusted since I was a teenager, when I first began asking the universe for answers. I had always been drawn to the "invisible": astrology, clairvoyance, energy. I used to hide that part of me. Now I know: it's the core of who I am.

I didn't create this system because I had all the answers. I developed it because I could no longer ignore the dissonance. I was successful on the outside but hollowed out on the inside. No matter how hard I worked, it always felt like I was pushing against something unseen.

Once I began honoring my energetic blueprint—instead of overriding it—everything shifted.

The Astrologer's Insight

On April 25, 2023, I sat across from my astrologer—a man I had trusted for nearly a decade. He looked at my chart and said, "You're not meant to lead the way others do. You're supposed to create your own system."

That conversation cracked something open. Not just an insight, but a remembering.

I nodded, made a note, and kept going. I thought he was referring to ReyRey, the sustainable fashion brand I had founded with soul, story, and strategy. That was the vision, and in many ways, it still is. However, something else was forming—a more introspective truth I hadn't yet dared to name.

He told me I would create a new system. Yet what he really gave me that day was an inner trigger that cracked up all that is unfolded in this book.

Then he said something that would prove prophetic in ways I couldn't yet understand: "If your timing is right, within three years, your career will shift dramatically. It will come suddenly—like lightning from a clear sky."

When the Frequency Says No

Months passed. I kept refining ReyRey. Kept striving.

In early January 2025, I was offered 14 million DKK in investment to scale the company. The kind of opportunity most founders dream of. Everything looked right, but something in me said no. Not softly. Not subtly. It screamed.

And I listened.

This wasn't the first time I had felt that knowing. The pattern had been revealing itself across decades, each instance teaching me to trust what my body understood before my mind could rationalize it.

In my mid-twenties, I lived through one of the most exhausting and disorienting periods of my life. For more than two years, no matter how much help or intervention I sought, conception did not happen. Each attempt ended in the same silence. Over time, that absence hollowed me out. I no longer felt normal. I no longer felt like a woman. At times, I no longer felt like a human being. It was as if life itself refused to move through me.

At the time, I believed something in me was broken. Only years later did I understand that what felt like failure was not biology gone wrong, but rather a matter of alignment at work. My body was not passive; it was precise. It was holding a boundary I could not yet name: This is not your timing. This is not your path.

I don't even remember if I finally listened to that instinctive knowing consciously. In 2012, I walked away from the life I had put together and the self I had outgrown. I ended a thirteen-year relationship, left the structure of my old world behind, and stepped into the unknown. It was here that things began to shift dramatically.

When I met the man who would later become my husband, I told him I could not have children—that I had tried everything and failed. Miraculously, life had a different plan. Without treatment, without effort, without even expectation, I conceived.

What had once seemed impossible unfolded with ease. What more than two years of force and intervention could not achieve happened naturally when alignment was present. My body, which had once closed every door, suddenly opened. Not because it was fixed, but because it was in cohesion.

While I'm writing this book, these experiences revealed something central to Frequency Intelligence: the body is a compass, uncompromising in its truth. It will withhold when the path is misaligned—no matter how much the mind resists—and it will open when coherence is found. What I once called brokenness, I now recognize as precision. The body itself is part of the frequency field—protective, intelligent, and exact in its timing.

Years later, in 2020, after nearly two years of negotiations, I had unintentionally ruined another significant investment opportunity. The discussions had been lengthy, detailed, promising—yet when it came time to surrender, my body contracted. The same inner signal would later guide me away from the 2025 funding.

The same sensation and the same inner certainty prevailed across all these pivotal moments. Still, no one understood—not even me, at first. Then something in me remembered.

It wasn't fear. It wasn't doubt. It was a more primal signal—a frequency. A form of knowing that didn't require words.

What I now recognize as Frequency Intelligence—before I had a name for it.

Looking back, I can see a pattern emerging across my life. Again and again, I had chosen alignment over approval. Truth over strategy. Frequency over force. Again and again, I had chosen inner pull over recognition, even when it made no logical sense, even when others couldn't understand the decision, even when I couldn't fully explain it to myself.

The Moment of Remembering

Saying no to that funding made no sense. It broke every rule I had once lived by. For weeks after, I felt empty, off-center, uncertain. I regretted it at times. How could I say no to this? However, my body knew: continuing down that path would cost me something I couldn't get back.

The moment I turned down that funding wasn't sabotage—it wasn't fear or self-destruction. It was a sacred clearing. A reset. A return to the chord that mattered. Because that "no" created space for a more resounding "yes." One that came not from strategy—but from soul. Not from what I should build, but from what I was destined to create.

In late February 2025, I woke up at 5:25 a.m. and typed something into my phone that would change everything. An idea. A download. Not a plan—but a pulse. That's how Frequency Intelligence was born: not from strategy, but from soul.

I started writing. Mapping. Listening. My energy returned, and that's when I remembered his words. I went back to the recording of our final session. He had seen it before I did.

The Prophecy Revisited

That moment stayed with me—especially because he passed away in August 2023, just months after that conversation. I never got to tell him he was right.

He didn't just read my chart. He named my trajectory. He recognized the turning point before I had words for it.

Every time I sit down to write, to speak, to build this system—I think of him: quietly, gratefully because part of me knows he was part of this. He always saw the bigger pattern. This book is for him, and for anyone who's ever felt the ache of alignment—before they had language for it.

Quantum Timing

This is what I mean by Quantum Timing. You don't always understand the moment when it happens. Yet when you look back, the alignment is undeniable.

Saying no to the funding wasn't sabotage. It was a signal. A sacred pause. A clearing. A doorway into what I was actually here to build.

This is what Frequency Intelligence teaches you to do—not to chase timing, but to trust yours.

You didn't miss your moment. You were becoming it.

The Bridge Between Structure and Soul

While other teenagers were exploring parties or trying to fit in, I was asking the universe for answers.

At thirteen, I was already fascinated by astrology. At fourteen, I had my first clairvoyant session—asking about love, of course. But it wasn't just about romance. It was the beginning of a lifelong dialogue with the unseen: astrology, clairvoyance, numerology, energy, healing, tarot, and meditation.

These weren't "woo" to me. They were home.

Through every major transition in my life—from divorce to reinvention, from Milan to meeting rooms—these tools became my compass.

I also lived in the "real world." I innovated businesses. I advised organizations. I coached executives. I created sustainable products and led strategic launches. I navigated both the spiritual and the structural.

Somewhere in between, I began to realize the world was hungry for a bridge—a way to connect profound, intuitive wisdom with grounded, everyday leadership.

The Invisible Curriculum Roots of the System

What I didn't realize until much later was that the roots of this system were planted years earlier, woven throughout what I now call my invisible curriculum. This education happens not in classrooms but in the lived experience of seeking alignment in a world that often demands the opposite.

In 2008, during my master's thesis, I was already asking questions about identity, values, and alignment. The paper was titled *The Green Wave*. It explored how sustainability and conscious consumption were becoming reflections of our inner values—not just market trends.

I argued that we were entering an era where buying wasn't about image. It was about awareness. That alignment—not performance—was the new aspiration.

How we live, lead, and consume must reflect who we truly are— not just what we want others to see.

In many ways, that was the beginning of Frequency Intelligence. Even then, I sensed a shift: It wasn't just about fashion. It was about frequency. I just didn't know the system had a name yet.

Now, years later, I see that my journey through burnout, reinvention, and energetic attunement was building on that foundation all along. Everything I had lived—my work in strategy, branding, entrepreneurship, personal reinvention, and spiritual practice—was the invisible curriculum that taught me how to build Frequency Intelligence. Not through theory, but through lived experience.

From Quantum Frequency to Frequency Intelligence

In the earliest journal entries—before this system had form—I called it Quantum Frequency. It was a placeholder. A whisper. The first language I used to describe what I was feeling.

I didn't yet understand what it would become, but I could feel it. Only later—after integrating astrology, numerology, emotional patterns, biofeedback, and AI—did I realize what I was building.

Not just a vision. Not just a product. But a new metaphysical operating system for how we live, create, and lead.

And now, that whisper has a name: Frequency Intelligence.

What Frequency Intelligence Really Is

This is not just an app or a methodology: it's a comprehensive solution. It is an energetic revolution—a metaphysical operating system designed for the modern human. It's a bridge between soul and science, between ancient codes and advanced technology.

It integrates astrology, numerology, biofeedback, neuroscience, emotional cycles, and AI-generated insights to guide you into alignment with your natural frequency—the rhythm already living inside your biology, birth chart, and inner compass.

This system doesn't push you to hustle harder. It shows you how to move in flow with the energetic and biological rhythms that are already shaping your life.

It's not about doing more. It's about doing what's right for you—at the right time.

This is the shift: from burnout to energetic sovereignty, from randomness to rhythm, from force to alignment.

You don't need to become someone else. You only need to remember who you already are.

 We're entering a new era. The old models are breaking down.

Hustle is being replaced by wholeness. Profit-at-all-costs is being questioned. Success is being redefined—not just by how it looks, but by how it feels.

Yet most tools, systems, and structures still treat humans like machines: we're given timelines that ignore timing, strategies that ignore the soul, tactics that ignore truth.

Frequency Intelligence flips the script.

It helps you work with your own rhythm, not against it. It prevents burnout instead of glorifying it. It doesn't guess—it guides.

This isn't about optimization. It's about remembrance.

Because the truth is, we were not created to live out of sync with ourselves.

This book is for the following people:

- Visionaries building the future
- Burnt-out leaders ready for a new path

- Entrepreneurs who are tired of guessing

- Seekers craving alignment

- Creatives, coaches, and changemakers who want a soul-led life—with structure

Whether you're deeply spiritual or highly strategic, this book meets you where you are—and invites you into something more meaningful: a life mapped by frequency, not by force.

How to Read This Book

Let's get one thing clear:

This isn't a spiritual book. It's a system—a living system that merges ancient intelligence with modern insight.

It's mapped to help you understand your energetic rhythm, lead from internal alignment, and make decisions from clarity and legacy tone—not confusion.

It's not based on belief. It's rooted in pattern recognition, biometric feedback, energetic timing, ancient wisdom systems, and modern technology.

You've heard of IQ (intellectual intelligence) and EQ (emotional intelligence).

This book introduces a new approach: FQ—Frequency Intelligence. A deeper layer of intelligence that helps you sync your timing, optimize your energy, lead from coherence, and align action with your inner truth

You can use this book in multiple ways: Read it cover to cover as a transformational journey. Return to specific chapters as a reference for the phase you're in. Integrate it with the Frequency Intelligence app and future wearable for real-time guidance.

Let it unfold in your rhythm—not someone else's.

What's Inside This Book

This isn't a self-help book. It's a map.

A field guide for living in energetic congruence with yourself: mentally, physically, emotionally, and cosmically.

Inside, you'll discover your Frequency Blueprint™: the energetic rhythm encoded in your birth chart, biology, and behavioral patterns.

It's not anchored on guesswork. It's grounded in data, cycles, and deep pattern recognition—both ancient and modern.

You'll learn the following:

- How to understand your personal energetic phases
- Track your creative highs and emotional dips
- Recognize when it's time to initiate, integrate, or reflect
- Make decisions from alignment, not pressure
- Lead with sovereign rhythm—in your business, your body, and your being

A System Born From Experience–Not Theory

This framework didn't emerge solely through research. It arrived through resistance. Through disruption. Through the deep remembering that comes after breakdown.

No amount of success ever made me feel whole—until I stopped chasing systems that ignored my rhythm.

That's when this system revealed itself.

Not in one flash, but in patterns, insights, repeated questions, and quiet clarity.

I didn't build this because I had everything figured out. I built it because I needed it.

And now, I offer it to you.

The Turning Point Was Never a Breakdown— It Was a Recalibration

We're taught to fear the pause. To rush through resistance. To hustle through doubt.

Yet what if the discomfort isn't a detour? What if it's a doorway? The moment I turned down 14 million DKK wasn't sabotage. It wasn't fear. It was a sacred clearing—a reset, a return to vibrational truth.

Because that "no" created space for a wholehearted "yes."

One that came not from strategy—but from soul. Not from what I should build, but from what I was intended to create.

That "yes" was Frequency Intelligence.

A Legacy Written in Sky, Not in Stone

I'll never forget the astrologer who saw this shift before I could.

He told me, "If your timing is right, everything will change— quickly. Like lightning from a clear sky."

He didn't just read my chart. He read my life. He mirrored a truth I hadn't yet remembered.

He passed away just a few months later. I never got to tell him he was right.

Now his voice lives in this book. His insight shaped its origin.

This is more than a tool or a system. It's a remembrance—so you can begin to return to yourself.

You Attract What You're Ready For

You don't attract what you want. You attract what you're aligned with.

And sometimes that means releasing what's "almost right" to make space for what's fully resonant.

That's what happened when Frequency Intelligence arrived—not as a strategy but as a pulse.

A download. A code. A system that felt both ancient and futuristic at once.

Because we don't invent these truths—we remember them.

They've been living inside us—unseen but never absent, encoded in our nervous system, written in our rhythms, waiting for the moment we stop overriding what we've always known.

If You're Holding This Book, You're Already In It

You don't need to become someone else. You don't need more effort, more validation, more force.

You need vibrational pacing. You need clarity. You need your own frequency.

Frequency Intelligence isn't about adding more. It's about remembering what's already in you—and learning how to live, lead, and create from that place.

So take a breath. You're not late. You're on time.

Welcome to your rhythm. Welcome to the new intelligence.

Welcome to you.

CHAPTER 1

The World's Next Intelligence

Frequency Intelligence (FQ) is not a personality type, a cultural trend, or a new version of motivational theory. It doesn't belong to a particular belief system, gender, location, or generation. It points to something more foundational. Something deep. More essential. More human.

FQ is a next-generation human operating system—one that unifies thought, emotion, and internal perception into a coherent signal you can trust and act from. It's not about amplifying logic or heightening emotional awareness in isolation. It's about aligning your inner timing, clarity, and direction so your decisions reflect not just what you think or feel—but what's fundamentally true for you in that moment.

Because long before the mind understands, the body knows. Because truth often arrives in stillness, not in noise. Because energy holds coherence, even when words cannot.

And in a world obsessed with speed, the ability to act from alignment—rather than reactivity—may be our last remaining power source.

These aren't passing trends. They're laws of being. The unspoken forces behind how we move, decide, burn out, break through, and find our way back to ourselves.

Now, after decades of intellectual and emotional development, it's time to name what has always been there—running in the background: a third form of intelligence.

One that governs timing, bandwidth, and inner attunement.

One that determines whether we are truly in sync with what we're doing or quietly collapsing under the surface of it all.

This is where Frequency Intelligence enters.

Over the past century, we've defined intelligence by our ability to think (IQ), feel (EQ), and adapt (AQ).

Yet one dimension has remained unmeasured: our ability to align.

FQ is not just another model. It's not a competitor in the intelligence hierarchy. It's a category shift.

It doesn't measure what you know or how you feel—it reveals when, why, and from where you act.

In a world spinning with overstimulation, algorithmic pressure, leadership fatigue, and inner collapse, that might be the most essential intelligence of all.

FQ is the intelligence of coherence in motion: It's how you make decisions when logic and emotion don't give you the whole picture. It's how you recognize when timing is off—even if everything "makes sense" on paper. It's how you move when the field is open, pause when it's not, and restore energy before your system crashes. IQ and EQ helped humanity evolve. However, they were built for structured, somewhat predictable environments—FQ was built for now.

Let's be clear—FQ doesn't replace the others, but without it, they eventually fail.

Because no matter how smart, strategic, or self-aware you are, if you're acting from misalignment, everything bends under pressure.

FQ is not a theory. It's a system-level intelligence that gives you access to the one thing no one else can define for you: your internal signal.

It is the next intelligence—not because it's new, but because we're finally ready to name it.

Intelligence Was Never Static

When psychologist Charles Spearman introduced the idea of "general intelligence" in the early 1900s, the IQ test became the dominant paradigm. Academic scores, cognitive tests, and rational problem-solving became the currency of competence. For much of the 20th century, IQ was the gold standard—and those who had it succeeded in structured, stable environments.

In the 1990s, psychologists Peter Salovey and John D. Mayer introduced the concept of emotional intelligence (EI), commonly known as EQ: the capacity to recognize, understand, and manage emotions in ourselves and others. Later, Daniel Goleman helped bring EQ to the mainstream, reframing leadership, business, and education. EQ shifted us from machines to humans.

But now? Neither is enough.

IQ and EQ were conceived for a world of relative predictability.

However, today's world is defined by interruption, acceleration, and energetic overload.

What happens when a brilliant mind burns out? Or when an emotionally attuned leader absorbs so much noise, they lose access to clarity?

Enter FQ—the intelligence that governs your energetic clarity, internal signal, and timing.

FQ is not a mood or a vibe. It's the capacity to read yourself and the room, track internal signals before breakdown, and move in attunement with what actually wants to emerge.

It's not vague intuition. It's patterned, practical, and deeply functional.

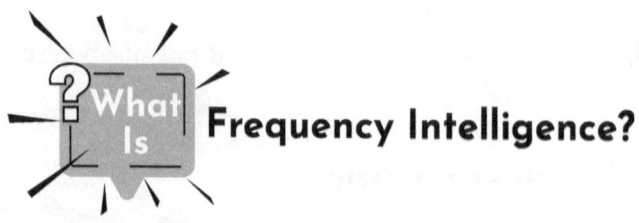

Frequency Intelligence?

Frequency Intelligence (FQ) is the capacity to read, interpret, and act from your own energetic state—even in a noisy or misaligned environment.

It's not about emotion. It's not about thought. It's about signal match.

FQ asks, "What energy are you operating from—and how well does it match the timing, context, and reality you're in?"

When you operate with high FQ, you can:

Know when to act and when to pause	Feel misalignment before it becomes a crisis	Lead without force—and still move mountains
Course-correct before burnout	Trust your signal more than external validation	

FQ doesn't rely on personality tests, identity labels, or self-improvement ideals. It draws from your current frequency—moment by moment.

Why IQ and EQ Fail Without FQ

You can be brilliant—and still self-destruct if your energy is wrong. You can be compassionate—and still collapse if you ignore your timing.

FQ is the silent variable behind why so many leaders, creatives, and changemakers get stuck. They don't lack intelligence or empathy.

They lack energetic clarity.

They've been taught to push through, override their signals, and force their way through the world rather than aligning with it.

Imagine this:

A high-IQ founder launches a visionary product at the wrong time—and it fails.

A high-EQ teacher holds space for others—until their own nervous system gives out.

A high-achieving woman does everything "right"— but feels an internal hollowness she can't explain.

These aren't character flaws. They're FQ failures.

When your frequency is misaligned, your outcomes become distorted. Your ideas fall flat. Your body resists. Your energy leaks. FQ brings the missing logic of energetic alignment back into the picture.

This isn't a soft skill. It's a precision tool.

Energetic Literacy *The New Non-Negotiable*

FQ is no longer optional. It's the foundation beneath sustainable performance, resilient leadership, and energetic curcuitry.

It helps you:

- Detect energetic dissonance before it becomes burnout
- Know when your "yes" is real—and when it's people-pleasing
- Use timing as a strategy—not superstition
- Align your actions with your actual system—not the noise of others
- Restore energy before it needs to be rescued

This isn't "trust your gut" advice. It's system-level human technology—backed by timing, rhythm, and real-world results.

FQ lets you move through life on signal. Not perfectly. Not always peacefully. But clearly, and in tune with who you are.

Real-World Signs of High FQ

You don't wait for a breakdown to adjust—you track subtle shifts. You don't guess—you listen. Your body is part of the data. You move when your system says yes—and rest before you're forced to.

You recognize when someone's energy is mismatched to their words—and you don't take it personally. You launch when the field is open. You reflect when clarity is needed.

You pause—not out of laziness, but because it's not time yet.

That's FQ in action. It's subtle, but it saves years.

Why This Intelligence Had No Name— Until Now

For decades, this intelligence wasn't just unnamed. It was unknown. It wasn't ignored. It was invisible. Not because it didn't exist, but because we lacked the awareness to recognize it.

The system was always running: in the background of our decisions, breakthroughs, burnouts, and inner signals. However, we didn't know how to name it.

It's like a button that's always been there, but no one told us it existed, or how to press it.

What we need now to call Frequency Intelligence has been guiding us all along.

It governed our timing, our misfires, our clarity, our collapses—silently aligning or misaligning our actions behind the scenes.

So now, we name it.

Because when you can name it, you can train it. And when you can train it, you can trust it.

FQ isn't just a new label. It's a new literacy: for how to live, lead, and sustain ourselves in a non-linear world.

Human Sustainability *The Forgotten Frontier*

Before FQ, I built ReyRey—a sustainable fashion brand with elegant, ethical shoes. I thought I was helping the planet, and I was. Yet I missed something: we can't build sustainable systems on unsustainable humans.

It doesn't matter how ethical your product is if the founder is burned out. It doesn't matter how green your building is if the team inside is energetically collapsed. It doesn't matter how many wellness initiatives you implement if the system still runs on push, override, and exhaustion.

We've been designing for the planet, not for the person.

FQ is human sustainability. It's inner climate regulation. It's nervous system intelligence. It's energy as data.

FQ asks:

?	**?**	**?**
What if burnout isn't a personal failure but a systemic feedback loop?	What if misalignment isn't weakness but misused timing?	What if our frequency is the real infrastructure that needs upgrading?

This isn't soft. It's strategic.

And it might be the most overlooked key to performance, leadership, and planetary recovery.

 We're living in a breakdown era.

- Burnout is at an all-time high and still rising.

- Productivity is optimized, but meaning is missing.

- Tech is advancing faster than our nervous systems can adapt.

- AI is replacing tasks but not embodiment.

- Strategy is outpacing clarity.

- Climate change is an outer mirror of our inner depletion.

In short, IQ is overclocked, and EQ is overloaded, and the system can't go faster.

We don't need better performance hacks. We need alignment literacy.

FQ gives you that—a way to feel, track, and act from your own internal rhythm instead of being run by noise, urgency, or programming.

This is not a luxury. It's the future.

FQ is not just for coaches or creatives. It's for anyone navigating noise, pressure, and uncertainty in a post-linear world.

It's for:

- Leaders who can no longer fake alignment

- Parents raising children who feel everything

- Executives who know strategy isn't enough

- Healers and helpers who've stopped healing themselves

- Logical high performers who feel lost—not because they're wrong, but because the system they erected no longer resonates

It's also for:

People who keep saying "yes"—and keep collapsing	Visionaries who feel timing but can't explain it	Professionals who are tired of overriding what they know in their bones

FQ gives them a map.

FQ Is Not a Trend It's a Technology of Self

FQ isn't coaching. It's not wellness. It's not a vibe, and it's not for sale on a retreat poster. It's a technology of self-governance—anchored in emotional cadence, rhythm, and restoration.

Like IQ had tests. Like EQ had tools.

FQ has:

- Blueprints—your personal energetic profile based on birth timing, patterns, and cycles

- Flow Maps—to track when to launch, align, and reflect based on your rhythm

- Daily Tools—the FQ Deck, the Frequency Journal, and soon, wearables and AI integration

- Energetic Literacy—the skill of spotting misalignment before it becomes a crisis

More than anything, FQ is practical:

Know your signal.

Live from that signal.

Adjust when the signal shifts.

This is not the future of spirituality. It's the future of performance, leadership, parenting, creation, and humanity.

We are entering a world where frequency literacy will define sustainability—not just for ecosystems—but for every system we live and lead within.

FQ is not a concept. It is the world's next intelligence.

CHAPTER 2

Why Frequency Intelligence in a World of AI?

We're standing at a threshold where technology now thinks faster than we do.

Artificial intelligence can write speeches, solve problems, and mimic human empathy with startling precision. The question isn't whether AI will continue to evolve—it will. The real question is *what becomes of us in that process?*

The fear isn't about robots taking over. It's quieter than that.

It's the slow erosion of human self-trust. The gradual outsourcing of our own timing, clarity, and decisions to systems that move faster but know us less.

That future only happens if we let it.

If we quietly hand over the control panel with all the buttons that make us human—then we let the algorithm take over the functions that used to live inside us: perception, intuition, timing, discernment, and choice.

I've seen both sides of this shift. I learned technology—I wasn't born into it. I still remember what it felt like to live off-screen, to move through time without constant notifications, and to make decisions that came from instinct rather than input.

That contrast is why I can see what the newer generations often cannot: The subtle shift from being human to outsourcing human. From living life to curating it. From sensing your own "yes" to checking a feed to decide how to feel.

That's the real danger—not AI itself.

It's the quiet loss of our ability to hear ourselves, trust ourselves, and lead from within.

We've all seen the metaphor before—a control panel inside the human mind.

In the film *Inside* Out, it's animated with emotion and memory, a playful representation of the internal mechanics that guide our choices and feelings.

Now imagine if that panel—your inner dashboard of truth, timing, and knowing—was quietly handed over to machines. Not just to support you, but to start deciding for you: what matters, what you should feel, when you should act.

That's not science fiction anymore. It's the reality we're drifting toward: subtle, sophisticated, and silent.

This is precisely why Frequency Intelligence exists.

Because in a world where control panels can be engineered, we must practice sovereignty.

Because in a world of accelerating code, the most valuable human skill will not be optimization—it will be self-resonance.

The ability to move not from noise, but from knowing.

To pause—not because an app reminds you, but because your body speaks first. To lead—not from reaction, but from rhythm.

FQ isn't here to compete with AI. It's here to preserve what no machine can simulate: the deep, embodied integrity of your own signal.

What Technology Can Do– and What It Can't

AI can reflect you—but it cannot regulate you.

It can mimic insight, but it cannot feel when your "yes" is real, or when it's actually a quiet "no." It can amplify your words, but it cannot embody your signal or track your timing.

That's the gap FQ was programmed to fill.

Not as another tool to optimize your habits, but as an inner operating framework—a system for decoding your own energy in real time.

A literacy of your own life force.

What FQ Actually Does

Where AI offers external advice, FQ builds internal coherence.

It doesn't just tell you to trust yourself: it teaches you how to feel when you're aligned, and how to recognize when you've drifted.

FQ helps you:

- Feel the difference between force and flow
- Catch subtle energetic misalignments before they lead to burnout
- Navigate timing by signal, not pressure
- Discern real intuition from fear, performance, or anxiety
- Build energetic sovereignty—the kind that doesn't collapse in overstimulation

It's not a motivational concept. It's a somatic system.

It trains you to track the state of your frequency—moment by moment—before your mind even starts to explain it.

FQ is your ability to feel what's true before it's validated: To pause when the world pushes. To act when your signal aligns—not just when your to-do list says it's time.

The Crisis of Clarity

As the volume of the world increases, nervous systems are struggling to cope with the weight of constant input.

People are performing identities instead of living from their inner truth.

Even well-intentioned leaders are burning out—not because they're unwise, but because they've lost their original rhythm.

AI is accelerating.

Success is no longer rare, but embodiment is. People are reaching goals, but they no longer feel alive in them.

So the real premium of the future will not be strategy or speed.

It will be:

Can you hear your own signal in the noise?	Can you trust your inner rhythm when the algorithm tells you to go?	Can you stay sovereign in a world that rewards reactivity?

AI + ChatGPT	Frequency Intelligence
External reflection	Internal alignment
Speed, synthesis, response	Embodiment, rhythm, integration
Intellect-driven	Nervous system attunement
High-functioning output	High-fidelity coherence
Answer machine	Energetic literacy system

No matter how advanced the technology becomes, it cannot embody your truth. It cannot sense when your system is out of rhythm.

It cannot feel what only you can feel.

What the App Actually Does

Yes, there's an FQ app, but it's not a chatbot.

It doesn't replace your decisions—it tunes your awareness. The app was developed to support sovereignty, not override it.

It gives you a way to:

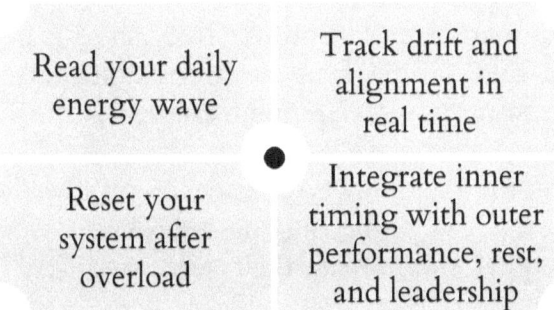

Read your daily energy wave

Track drift and alignment in real time

Reset your system after overload

Integrate inner timing with outer performance, rest, and leadership

It's not about making you more productive. It's about making you more present to what's real inside your system.

A Personal Reflection and a Universal Need

This chapter isn't theory. It's lived.

For years, I thought optimization was the path to freedom. If I could only move faster, organize more, do better—I would feel whole, but I didn't feel whole.

I felt effective, even successful, but I couldn't hear myself anymore.

FQ didn't arrive as a concept. It arrived as a necessity.

It gave me a language for what I had always sensed, but never knew how to name.

Now it's a system for others too: For those who want clarity without collapse. For those who have decided to stop outsourcing their timing. For those who are ready to take back the control panel—not from fear, but from truth.

The Future Is Not Anti-Tech *It's Pro-Human*

This work is not against technology. It's for human integrity within it. Because even in a world of flawless simulations, the one thing no machine can replicate is you.

Your rhythm. Your timing. Your felt sense of what's real.

FQ ensures that your decisions, leadership, parenting, and contribution don't come from compensation, performance, or pressure, but from clarity, alignment, and self-leadership.

In the future, the most powerful leaders won't be the ones who move the fastest. They'll be the ones who know when to pause, trust their signal more than their feed, and lead from tonal integrity—not reactivity.

The Signal Was Always Yours

This isn't just about reading a new concept. It's about remembering what was always yours: That intelligence isn't just in your mind—it's in your body. That clarity isn't just in strategy—it's in frequency.

Your timing isn't an app alert—it's a living wave inside you.

You're not behind. You're right on time, and so is this system.

Frequency Intelligence isn't just about keeping up with the future.

It's about making sure your humanity comes with you.

CHAPTER 3
Generational Repair

Every generation carries both wisdom and wounds.

Sometimes, what we inherit is unspoken—a quiet, yet powerful, emotional survival strategy passed down through culture. Other times, it's loud: visible in the expectations placed on us, the systems we grow up in, and the technologies we receive before we know how to use them. Whether silent or screaming, these patterns shape us, and often, they keep us from hearing ourselves clearly.

This is where Frequency Intelligence becomes more than a personal tool. It becomes a form of generational repair.

When you learn to read your own energy—your real yes, your quiet no, your internal rhythm—you aren't just healing your life. You're interrupting a lineage of unconscious patterns. You're ending the loop. You're restoring something that was lost generations ago: energetic sovereignty.

Let's look at how we got here.

The Generational Pattern

Baby Boomers (1946-1964)
Born into the aftermath of war, this generation was shaped by the need for survival, structure, and security. Hard work and external achievement became their emotional armor. Vulnerability wasn't just discouraged—it was unsafe.

They created the world we inherited: corporate hierarchies, institutional frameworks, systems of measurement, and reward. They valued consistency, loyalty, and linear progression. Yet in their focus on external security, they often lost connection to internal guidance.

Their shadow side: They disconnected from their inner world in favor of performance and status, often equating self-worth with productivity.

FQ Restores Inner Literacy, so success is defined by alignment, not image.

Generation X (1965-1980)
Often raised by emotionally distant or overworked parents, many became the "latchkey kids."

They grew up with early independence, but without emotional attunement. They learned not to trust systems—or sometimes, even connections.

This generation witnessed the breakdown of many institutional promises that their parents believed in. They witnessed corporate layoffs, divorce rates climb, and traditional structures prove unreliable. Their response was often cynicism and radical self-reliance.

Their shadow side: Self-reliance gave rise to emotional isolation. Skepticism hardened into disconnection.

FQ Restores Energetic Connection: so independence doesn't require isolation.

Millennials (1981-1996)
Told they could "be anything," millennials were dreamers raised inside outdated systems.

They were encouraged to follow their passion, yet still judged by material milestones. Add to that the explosion of digital culture, social media, and nonstop comparison.

This generation was promised that hard work and education would lead to prosperity, but they entered a job market that didn't deliver on those promises. They responded by questioning everything: traditional career paths, relationship models, and definitions of success.

However, they still carried the pressure to achieve, now amplified by the visibility and comparison on social media.

Their shadow side: Constant performance. Burnout beneath the polish. A feeling of emotional bankruptcy despite outward success.

FQ Restores Sovereign Timing: so they can choose impact over image, voltage over recognition.

Generation Z (1997-2012)

Born into a curated world, they never knew life without a screen. They are fluent in emotional vocabulary but lack the embodied tools to ground it. They know how to describe their anxiety, but not how to metabolize it.

This generation has unprecedented access to information about mental health, social justice, and global issues. They can articulate complex emotional states and systemic problems with remarkable precision. Yet this awareness often comes without the embodied practices to process what they know.

They feel everything—climate anxiety, social injustice, economic uncertainty. That said, they were never taught how to transform feeling into sustainable action or how to protect their energy while staying engaged with the world's pain.

Their shadow side: Overstimulated but under-rooted.

Hyperaware, but energetically fragile.

FQ Restores Frequency-Based Resilience: so they can feel deeply without collapsing.

This generation will never know a world without AI.

Their lives are tracked, optimized, and data-managed before they can even form conscious memory. Their toys talk. Their moods are predicted. Their choices are filtered.

They're growing up with technology that adapts to them before they learn to adapt to themselves. Algorithms predict their preferences before they develop their own taste. Their attention is managed by systems constructed to capture it.

Their risk: Living as avatars of themselves—disconnected from a core they never had time to hear.

FQ Offers an Energetic Navigation System: so they can find their own internal compass in a world of external noise.

Where the Chain Broke

With every generation, collective awareness expanded:

We got better at naming trauma.	We became more emotionally articulate.	We began to question outdated norms.

Nevertheless, we never developed an authentic system for energetic literacy.

What we were never taught:

How to feel our own frequency	How to regulate energy—not just thoughts	How to move from inner timing rather than outer pressure

Each generation developed different coping mechanisms for the same underlying disconnection from internal guidance. Boomers worked harder. Gen X detached. Millennials optimized. Gen Z articulated. Yet none were taught to listen to the signal beneath the noise.

This is the missing link. This is what FQ restores.

Not just understanding, but embodiment. Not just healing, but realignment.

A Personal Reflection

I know this pattern because I've lived it.

As the daughter of Iranian parents with big dreams and even bigger expectations, I was raised with a roadmap that defined success through achievement. I learned what kind of education I should have, what kind of job to pursue, what kind of car to drive, what sort of man to love—all before I ever learned to ask what I actually wanted.

For years, I couldn't tell the difference between my desires and the ones that had been handed to me. I didn't know which emotions were my own and which had been absorbed from others. I wasn't ignoring myself—I just didn't know who that self was beneath the layers of expectation, culture, and noise.

The Iranian culture I was raised in valued education, achievement, and outward success as markers of worth and security. These weren't wrong values, but they were incomplete. They addressed survival needs without acknowledging the soul's needs for authentic expression and internal modulation.

My parents had immigrated to create better opportunities, carrying both the dreams and traumas of displacement. They passed down their hopes along with their fears—the belief that hard work would create security, but also the anxiety that security could never be fully trusted.

FQ gave me a way back—a way to hear myself again.

Now, it's becoming the map for others—not just to survive their conditioning, but to choose something new.

Cultural Healing Patterns

Different cultural backgrounds create specific patterns of frequency dimension emphasis or suppression:

Achievement-oriented cultures often emphasize mental dimension development while suppressing emotional intelligence and spiritual consideration that don't translate into measurable success.

Collectivist traditions may unconsciously suppress the expression of individual spiritual dimensions in favor of group harmony, while simultaneously offering strong community support for emotional processing and healing.

Immigrant families frequently carry both survival-focused achievement pressure and cultural displacement trauma that affects how natural rhythms and spiritual practices are valued or dismissed.

Religious conditioning creates complex relationships with spiritual dimension expression, sometimes enhancing connection to transcendent intelligence while creating shame around personal spiritual authority.

Understanding these patterns allows for more precise healing approaches that honor cultural gifts while releasing limitations.

Summary Table

Generation	Cultural Pattern	Core Shadow	What FQ Restores
Baby Boomers	Achievement = safety	Emotional suppression	Inner literacy
Generation X	Self-reliance, distrust of systems	Isolation, emotional detachment	Energetic connection
Millennials	Passion + performance pressure	Burnout, identity exhaustion	Sovereign timing
Generation Z	Awareness without embodiment	Hyperstimulation, fragility	Frequency-based resilience
Generation Alpha	Full AI integration, no inner compass	Fragmented identity, digital self	Energetic navigation system

This Is a Bridge, Not a Break

You are not just building a system for today. You are closing a loop that's been open for generations.

You are offering what was never offered before: a way to reclaim self-leadership—not just for individuals, but for entire family lines.

FQ is not a reaction—it is a restoration.

Not a rejection of progress—but a recalibration of what it means to be human inside it.

It's the bridge between survival and sovereignty.

Between inherited pain and chosen alignment.

Between what we were given and what we now get to give.

This represents a fundamental shift from adapting ourselves to inherited systems that may not serve our authentic expression, to creating new systems that honor both individual energetic truth and collective well-being.

When you develop frequency literacy, you don't just heal your own patterns—you become a bridge for others who are ready to break cycles of energetic disconnection that may have been passed down for generations.

This is generational repair, and it starts with you.

CHAPTER 4

The Frequency Blueprint

Before we move into the Frequency Blueprint, it's important to clarify something: Frequency Intelligence (FQ) is bigger than astrology, numerology, or any single tool.

These systems are lenses. Astrology maps cosmic timing.

Numerology decodes vibrational patterns. Blueprinting organizes flow into Launch, Align, and Reflect. They are useful instruments, but they are not the intelligence itself.

FQ is the meta-intelligence that sits underneath them—just as IQ is not the same as mathematics, and EQ is not the same as therapy.

Math is a way to measure and grow cognitive intelligence (IQ).

Therapy is one way to expand emotional intelligence (EQ). But IQ and EQ exist regardless of the methods used.

In the same way, FQ is not dependent on astrology or numerology. These are instruments that reveal their patterns, not their definitions. Frequency Intelligence is your innate ability to sense timing, regulate energy, and act in alignment with your harmonic pulse.

This distinction matters. Without it, FQ could be misunderstood as another spiritual practice. It is not. It is a category of intelligence in its own right—as essential to future leadership and human sustainability as IQ and EQ have been to the past.

And that brings us here—to the Frequency Blueprint, the framework that makes this invisible intelligence visible.

Up until now, I have shared the background, the awakening, and the recognition that something more elemental was guiding my path—even when I didn't yet have language for it. But a system only becomes real when it moves beyond story and into structure.

The question I kept circling was that if alignment is real—if frequency is real—how do we map it? How do we turn whispers and signals into something you can see, follow, and trust?

Chapter 4 is where I finally name it. This is the moment when the threads of intuition, astrology, science, and lived experience converge into something clear. Not just insight, not just reflection, but a blueprint—a design that explains not only why I felt misaligned for so long, but how every one of us can live in sync with the rhythm we were born with.

Misalignment in the Midst of Success

It's a difficult thing to describe: the subtle dissonance that lingers beneath a life that looks right on paper. I wasn't unhappy, exactly. I wasn't failing. In fact, I was succeeding by almost every conventional measure. The brand was growing. The invitations were arriving. The recognition was real. I had molded something that the world responded to with applause—and yet, I was incapable of receiving it.

I don't mean that I was ungrateful. I was moved, even proud at times. Yet the response didn't land in me the way I had expected it would. It floated just outside my nervous system, like light passing through glass. I could see it. I could name it. Still, I couldn't feel it. Not in the way that matters—not in the place where joy anchors.

For the most part, I feel joy in my stomach. That quiet warmth. That expanding sense of something being right. Whole. Alive. Yet what I felt instead was a subtle flatness—a performance of reception, without the inner arrival. I would smile. I would say thank you. I would celebrate the milestone. Then almost immediately, I'd think, *What's next?*

That became the loop. Achieve. Acknowledge. Advance. I kept hoping the upcoming launch would deliver that internal click. That the next product would awaken the feeling I hadn't yet been able to access. Perhaps this time, I'd tell myself—perhaps now, *it will finally feel like enough.*

Though it never did, and I wasn't entirely conscious of this pattern at the time. I didn't know I was searching. I didn't see that I was reaching. I only knew that something was missing—but I didn't know that I knew it. That's the strangest part about misalignment: we can feel the ache long before we have the language for it.

Now I understand.

I wasn't building from joy. I was building toward it. I was creating from a place of internal dissonance—hoping the external result would resolve it. In reality, alignment doesn't work like that. It cannot be outsourced. It cannot be earned through applause.

Alignment must be felt in real time, not post-achievement.

That's what the Frequency Blueprint finally gave me. Not a set of traits or personality types—but a map back to the rhythm I had always sensed yet never fully trusted. It didn't tell me who I was. It showed me where I had been out of step with who I had always been.

You Weren't Born to Blend In

You weren't born to blend in. You were born to broadcast.

There's a reason you've always felt a little different—more sensitive, more intuitive, more attuned to undercurrents other people missed. It's not because you're fragile. It's because you were born to feel. Not emotionally—energetically.

Your life isn't random. It's rhythmic.

At the core of Frequency Intelligence is a simple, radical truth: you were born with an energetic blueprint. Not a personality type. Not a productivity model. A cosmic, physiological, and emotional map—a code—detailing how your physical, emotional, mental, and spiritual systems move through time, decision-making, relationships, and purpose.

Most people have never seen theirs. They live by default, not by design.

I did too.

I followed what made sense. I created companies. Hit milestones. Earned visibility. I brought into existence things the world celebrated. Just the same, those things often felt empty. I made decisions that looked right and felt wrong. I launched at times when everything should've worked—but didn't.

For years, I couldn't understand why my efforts never quite landed. Why something always felt slightly off—even in success.

The Turning Point: April 25, 2023

The turning point came in April 2023, when I sat across from my astrologer—a man I had trusted for nearly a decade—and he mirrored my life back to me in a way I had never experienced.

He didn't just interpret my birth chart. He translated my soul.

He named patterns I had never been able to articulate. He traced the energetic cycles behind my breakdowns and breakthroughs. He showed me that what I thought were failures … were actually misaligned timing.

Suddenly, the past fifteen years made sense. It wasn't randomness. It was rhythm.

What's more, that moment didn't just give me insight. It gave me permission—permission to stop fighting the current. Permission to listen differently. Permission to live by your current, not resistance.

However, what he said next would prove to be prophetic.

"You're going to create something in the next three years that will change everything," he told me, looking directly at my chart. "It won't come from pressure. It'll come like lightning from a clear sky. If your timing is right, everything will shift—quickly."

At the time, I thought he meant ReyRey. I nodded and moved on, but that moment cracked something open. Not just an insight, but a remembering.

He passed away just a few months later in August 2023. I never got to tell him he was right, but his voice lives in this book. His insight shaped its origin. Because now I know: he didn't just read my chart. He named my future before I could see it myself.

Looking back now, I see that my path had been whispering this system to me for years. I just hadn't been fluent in its language yet.

The Blueprint You Were Born With

When people ask what Frequency Intelligence actually does, I often tell them this: It doesn't teach you who to become. It helps you remember who you already are.

Your Frequency Blueprint is your soul's operating system. It governs how you respond to pressure, how you make aligned decisions, how your body processes energy, and when your system is wired to act, reflect, or recalibrate.

It's not a fixed identity. It's a living rhythm.

Through the Frequency Intelligence framework, your unique code is decoded into practical patterns—what we call your Flow Zones.

Each person cycles through three dominant energetic states:

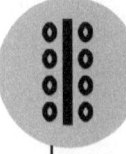

Launch— when your energy is geared toward creation, forward movement, and newness.

Align—when you integrate, recalibrate, deepen your awareness, and prepare.

Reflect— when you pause, process, and allow inner truths to rise.

You are always in one of these states. The key is knowing which one—and not forcing another.

When you move out of sync with your zone, the cost is high. You might experience burnout, resistance, confusion, or emotional shutdown. You may seek clarity from outside sources and feel increasingly disconnected from your own signal.

Whereas when you move with your frequency? That's when everything shifts.

What Happened in 2022

In 2022, I felt it again—that silent misalignment. I was running a visible, successful business. I had global recognition, but inside, I was irritated, restless, disconnected. The joy was gone. The creativity felt forced. Every move dragged as if I were pushing through sand.

I tried different strategies, reorganized projects, and even redesigned parts of the brand. Despite that, the frustration only deepened. Nothing flowed.

I wasn't in a creation zone. I wasn't in alignment for action or visibility. I was in a Reflect season—a period meant for inward focus, spiritual attunement, rest—but I was trying to Launch.

Fighting your energetic timing is like trying to sprint underwater.

The effort is real, but the impact is minimal. Everything resists. Nothing sustains.

When I surrendered to my blueprint, the friction stopped. I canceled a major collaboration. I paused product development. I stepped back from opportunities that looked brilliant on paper—but felt wrong in my body.

Afterward, slowly, I returned to my center. That pause didn't just save my energy. It made space for the download that would become Frequency Intelligence.

The Pulse Before the Blueprint

In early 2025, when I achieved the funding to scale ReyRey, it was everything I had worked for. Nevertheless, when I sat with the offer in my hands, something in my body said no. Not my mind— my mind screamed yes, but the signal wasn't in my logic.

It was in my frequency.

For weeks after, I was in free fall. Why did I say no? What was I thinking? Had I just sabotaged everything? I felt broken—like I had let something important slip away without knowing why. Yet, underneath the confusion … a space had opened.

In that space, something arrived. A pulse. A pattern. Not an idea. A knowing.

That knowing became Frequency Intelligence. It wasn't something I invented. It was something I remembered.

Later, I went back and listened to a recording from the April 2023 astrologer session. His words came flooding back: "If your timing is right, everything will change—quickly. Like lightning from a clear sky."

He had seen it before I did. That moment and his guidance stayed with me. Only now do I see it: he didn't just read my chart. He named my trajectory before I had words for it.

What Is the Frequency Blueprint?

Imagine if you had a map—a personal navigation system that showed you:

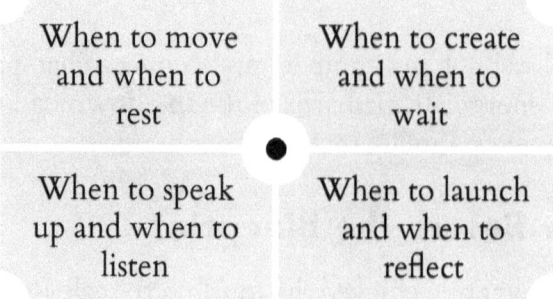

When to move and when to rest

When to create and when to wait

When to speak up and when to listen

When to launch and when to reflect

A system that reveals your energy highs, emotional lows, mental clarity peaks, and spiritual openings. Not conceptually—but with real-world data. As if you could see your energy as clearly as your calendar.

That's the Frequency Blueprint.

Your Frequency Blueprint isn't a personality test. It's a living, energetic map—a multidimensional intelligence system rooted in five primary layers:

Astrology	Numerology	Biological Rhythms
your cosmic architecture	your soul's vibrational timing	your embodied flow

Real-Time Feedback	Mental and Emotional Patterns
your internal climate	your living pulse

Each layer is powerful on its own, but the real intelligence lives in the intersection. That's where Frequency Intelligence is born. It's a biometric strategy system for your soul.

This is what your Frequency Blueprint reveals:

- Your dominant Flow Zone (Launch, Align, Reflect)

- Your natural timing for creation, rest, and recalibration

- Emotional patterns linked to planetary cycles

- Physical symptoms of misalignment

- Your unique energetic rhythm in relationships, leadership, and self-expression

The Four Core Layers of the Blueprint

Your Frequency Blueprint consists of four primary energetic systems that work together like interlocking gears. Each one provides a unique lens into your energy, purpose, timing, and potential. The power lies not in each layer alone—but in how they interact.

Your birth chart isn't just a horoscope. It's a sacred code—a snapshot of the sky at the moment you were born. It reveals:

- Your Sun sign—core identity

- Your Moon sign—emotional nature

- Your Rising sign—life path

- Your elemental makeup—fire, earth, air, water

- Your energy style—cardinal, fixed, mutable

- Planetary aspects and house placements that define your soul's path

Interestingly, this isn't static. Through AI, Frequency Intelligence tracks how current planetary transits activate your personal chart in real time.

Example: If Mars is opposing your natal Moon, your emotional energy may feel reactive or depleted. The system reads this and recommends stillness over action, reflection over projection.

Your birth chart becomes a dynamic GPS, not just a one-time reading.

Most people stop at "What's your sign?" when your chart is a blueprint for timing, energy, and expansion. Through AI, Frequency Intelligence doesn't just analyze your chart once. It tracks how current planetary transits (planetary movements) activate your personal placements—live.

Advanced Example: If Venus (planet of love) is squaring your natal Saturn (discipline), you may feel restriction in relationships that day. The app doesn't just tell you this—it suggests reflection over reaction. Stillness over action. Awareness over assumption.

Your chart becomes a living map, not just a personality description.

If astrology is the map, numerology is the clock.

Using your birthdate, numerology reveals:

- Life Path Number—the vibration of your soul's journey

- Personal Year—the theme of your current chapter

- Personal Month and Day—microcycles for decisions and energy

Each number carries a distinct frequency:

1 =Initiation, independence, courage

2 =Partnership, patience, intuition

3 =Creativity, expression, expansion

4 =Structure, building, foundation

5 =Freedom, change, adventure

6 =Nurturing, responsibility, harmony

7 =Introspection, spirituality, wisdom

8 =Power, achievement, material mastery

9 =Endings, release, transcendence

Numbers carry vibration. Your birth date reveals your Life Path Number (your soul's core direction), Personal Year (your theme for this year), and monthly and daily numbers (your microcycles). Numerology adds intuitive logic to your daily flow. It answers, "Is today a day to initiate or reflect? Launch or rest? Meet or retreat?" It gives structure to your inner signals.

Instead of guessing, you wake up to a precise energetic forecast: "Today is a 7 Day in a 1 Year. Go inward. Don't launch. Listen." That's vibrational precision.

Practical Application: "Today is a Personal 9 Day. Let go of something outdated. Don't force outcomes—complete instead."

Layer 3: Biological Rhythms—Your Embodied Flow
Your body knows, even when your mind doesn't.

The Frequency Blueprint integrates live physiological data:

- **Heart Rate Variability (HRV)**—shows stress and recovery

- **Sleep Quality**—your natural energy peaks and restoration needs

- **Hormonal Flow**—the biochemical tides that affect mood and energy

- **Stress Patterns**—your nervous system regulation

- **Movement and Rest Cycles**—how physical activity impacts your system

- **Biorhythms**—emotional, physical, and intellectual cycles following 23-, 28-, and 33-day patterns

This is where data meets intuition. We track Heart Rate Variability (HRV), sleep and movement patterns, nervous system regulation, and energy fluctuations—spikes and crashes—over time.

Your biological inputs are matched with cosmic signals. If your HRV is low and your transits indicate reflection, the system might say, "Do not pitch today. Walk. Breathe. Ground. Your next move will come tomorrow."

This is bio-intelligent leadership: Energy first. Strategy second.

Through wearable integration or manual tracking, Frequency Intelligence reads your biological signals and overlays them with your cosmic ones. If you've had poor sleep and you're in a low-energy moon transit, it won't tell you to hustle—it will tell you to regenerate.

Example: "Your emotional rhythm is in a low dip today—prioritize rest and emotional self-care. Avoid big relationship decisions."

With wearable integration, your body becomes part of the blueprint. You don't just read energy—you measure it.

Layer 4: Mental and Emotional Patterns – Your Inner Climate

Emotions are data. Thoughts are energy. Frequency Intelligence learns your internal cycles over time:

- When you feel depleted versus inspired
- What external triggers collapse your clarity
- What rituals restore your coherence
- Your patterns of mental fog versus sharp focus
- Creative surges and emotional dips

How you feel shapes how you flow. Over time, the system tracks your mood logs, thought patterns, and energy self-assessments.

The system doesn't treat your moods as noise. It treats them as clues. Over time, this evolves into precision coaching: from burnout to emotional fluency.

Frequency Intelligence learns your personal emotional cycles. It notices when you tend to feel low—before a full moon, after overworking, or during certain numerology days—and adjusts your guidance accordingly.

This turns your emotional life into intelligence, not interference.

The system also integrates neuro-coaching tools:

- Affirmations matched to your current state
- Journaling prompts customized for your energetic phase

- Breathwork patterns synced to your nervous system needs

- Frequency sound healing calibrated to your blueprint (396 Hz grounding tracks, binaural beats, solfeggio tones)

These aren't random—they're prescriptions matched to your energetic fingerprint.

Example: "Listen to your 396 Hz grounding track. Today is not the day to push forward. Reflect, reset, and wait."

With consistent data, Frequency Intelligence learns your personal cycles. You'll start to see patterns—emotional lows before New Moons, mental clarity on your 9-energy days, creative surges during fire sign transits.

The Quantum Frequency Formula

How the Blueprint Works

Your Frequency Blueprint is created by merging three data streams:

1. Astrology

Your natal chart offers a soul-level map of your natural rhythms, patterns, archetypes, and timing. It reveals when you're wired to act, rest, collaborate, create, or pull back.

2. Biofeedback

Through physiological data like Heart Rate Variability, skin temperature, cycle tracking, and sleep patterns, your nervous system tells us when you're in framework—or crisis.

3. Artificial Intelligence

By using pattern recognition and real-time inputs, AI becomes the translator. It doesn't override you—it reflects you. It notices patterns you may miss and synchronizes your blueprint with the life you're building.

When these three elements come together, they create what I call:

> **The Quantum Frequency Formula: Astrology + Biofeedback + AI = Real-Time Resonance.**

Ultimately, that is what this system is designed to deliver.

Beyond Static Insight

Most spiritual tools—whether astrology apps or daily horoscopes—offer insight but no real guidance. They tell you what's happening, but not how to shift it. The Quantum Frequency Formula changes that by providing a dynamic feedback system that merges metaphysical wisdom with real-time data science.

This isn't just a framework—it's a living intelligence system, drafted to empower you to regulate your life energetically, emotionally, and practically.

The Anatomy of Frequency

Everything in the universe has a frequency. Your thoughts. Your organs. Your DNA. Even your emotions vibrate at specific frequencies that can be measured and influenced.

The Quantum Frequency Formula is modeled on this foundational truth: your state of being is not random—it's responsive.

To clarify, if it's responsive, it can be designed, tracked, and optimized.

The Five Inputs of the Formula

Let's dive deeper into the five main components that feed the AI system's daily and weekly guidance:

1. Astrology: The Cosmic Clock

- The formula begins with your natal chart, which is calculated using your date, time, and place of birth.

- Then it compares planetary transits—the current positions of the planets—to show which themes are activated in your life.

- Personal Dashboard: The AI tells you, "You're entering a 3-day Mars period—perfect for launching, pitching, or high-energy work. Avoid impulsive arguments."

2. Numerology: Your Inner Timing

- Based on your Life Path Number (birthdate total) and Personal Year, Month, and Day Numbers, the AI knows which life cycle you're in.

- Personal Dashboard: "Today is a Personal 9 Day. Let go of something outdated. Don't force outcomes—complete instead."

3. Biorhythms: Your Biological Blueprint

- Uses your birth data to generate personal biorhythm curves—emotional, physical, and intellectual cycles (23/28/33-day patterns).

- Personal Dashboard: "Your emotional rhythm is in a low dip—prioritize rest and emotional self-care. Avoid big relationship decisions."

4. Biofeedback: Real-Time Energetic Insight

- HRV, stress levels, movement, and sleep tracking refine your energy state daily.

- Personal Dashboard: "Pause before your 3 p.m. meeting. Breathe. Neptune square Mars suggests confusion. Anchor into facts."

5. Neuro-Coaching Algorithms

- Pulls from psychology and CBT—generates personalized mantras, breathwork patterns, frequency audio (binaural beats, solfeggio tones), and mindset shifts.

- Personal Dashboard: "Listen to your 396 Hz grounding track. Today is not the day to push forward. Reflect, reset, and wait."

How the Blueprint Is Created

Creating your Frequency Blueprint is a three-step process that builds a comprehensive energetic profile:

Step 1: User Inputs

- Date, time, and place of birth (for astrological chart calculation)

- Full name and gender identity (for numerology profile)

- Optional biofeedback via wearable (for real-time physiological data)

- Initial energy and mood assessments (to establish baseline patterns)

Step 2: AI Analysis

- Integrates astrology, numerology, biological, and emotional data into a unified system

- Builds a custom energy map with phase-based insights

- Calculates optimal timing windows for different types of activities

- Generates personalized recommendations based on your current energetic climate

- The more you engage, the more accurate your blueprint becomes.

- Updates continuously with planetary movements and your real-time input.

- Learns your personal patterns and refines recommendations.

- Adapts to life changes and evolving circumstances.

The Flow Map: Your Inner Rhythm

For most of my life, I thought I had to push. That success came from output, momentum, and always staying ahead.

The truth is, I was trying to force a triangle into a square.

I burned energy. I drained myself. I delivered results, yes, while I often ignored my body's quiet voice. I worked in cycles, but I didn't know they had names until I discovered the Flow Map.

The Flow Map is how we move inside Frequency Intelligence. It's your inner rhythm. A cycle of three zones: Launch, Align, and Reflect.

You don't live at full speed all the time. Your mind, body, emotions, and soul all move in waves—just like the moon, the markets, the seasons.

The Three Flow Zones

Launch is the spark. The idea rush. The brainstorm that wakes you up at 3 a.m. In my body, it feels like a twister of energy—a storm of possibilities. When I'm in Launch, I don't need caffeine. I'm plugged in.

In Launch mode, you're envisioning, dreaming, sketching. You're not editing—you're downloading. This is the creative zone where

Frequency Intelligence can help you catch ideas before you second-guess them. You are inspired, electrified, and bursting with potential.

Best for: starting new projects, visibility, launching, pitching, public speaking, initiating change	You'll feel: confident, inspired, energized	AI Signal: "Mars trine Jupiter + Personal Year 1 = go big."

Align is where the action happens. You send the emails. Finalize the contracts. Create the product. It's not about hustle—it's about harmony. You're executing the right things at the right time. For me, Align feels like precision. The ship leaves the harbor. The right decisions land.

Align is often where people force themselves to live all the time. However, Align only works when preceded by true inspiration and followed by integration. Without the full cycle, even aligned action can lead to burnout.

Best for: recalibrating your path, course-correcting, updating vision	You'll feel: thoughtful, analytical, possibly unsure—but open	AI Signal: "Saturn is active. Focus on systems and long-term moves."

Reflect is the pause—the soft recalibration. The sacred inhale. This is the most misunderstood zone—especially for high achievers—but it's where the magic settles. You review. You rest. You let the universe catch up. When I'm in Reflect, I feel the question: What will actually manifest?

For years, I fought Reflect. I thought slowing down meant falling behind. That if I wasn't producing, I wasn't valuable. That's the old story.

Now I know—Reflect is the zone of buried wisdom. The insights that only come when you stop filling the silence. This is the zone where you recalibrate your energy bodies, reconnect with your values, and release anything not aligned.

Best for: letting go, journaling, spiritual work, recovery	**You'll feel:** tired, sensitive, introspective	**AI Signal:** "Neptune square Mercury + Personal Month 7 = step back and **reflect**."

Your Flow Map shows you which zone you're in on any given day, week, or month—and offers rituals, decisions, and guidance tailored to that energy.

The Cost of Misalignment

When you launch during a Reflect cycle, you lose momentum.

When you reflect during an Align cycle, you miss the window.

When you align during a Launch cycle, you build on a blurry vision.

I've lost money. Time. Energy. I've hired during an off-cycle and had to rebuild. I've said yes during the wrong phase and felt it cost me months of misalignment.

In contrast, when I trust the zone I'm in, everything flows. Writing this book has been my clearest example of this. It came out of me like water. I was in pure Launch. Pure fire. Even my kids noticed. Even my husband said, "You've never looked so focused. So sure." That's not willpower. That's frequency.

Reading Your Flow Through Astrology

Your astrological chart can help you know which zone you're most naturally inclined toward—and where you need support:

- **Mars or Aries energy?** You're a Launcher.

- **Virgo, Saturn, or Capricorn?** You're likely a natural Aligner.

- **Pisces, Neptune, or Moon dominant?** You are a Deep Reflector.

Frequency Intelligence helps decode these patterns and match them to your biometric flow. However, even on your own, noticing these rhythms enables you to reclaim self-trust.

Flow Map Metaphor
Think of the Flow Map like surfing:

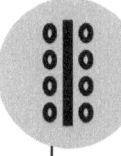

Launch—is paddling out, catching the wave.

Align—is riding it with focus and finesse.

Reflect—is letting the ocean bring you back to shore.

You wouldn't try to surf nonstop for the whole day. That's how most people treat their energy—and it's why they burn out.

Energy Phases and Flow Cycles

Your life moves in energetic seasons—not just in nature, but within your body, emotions, and cosmic timing. Frequency Intelligence helps you align your actions with your highest energetic phase.

There are three main cyclical systems we track:

Each month, the Moon moves through eight key phases, influencing your energy, focus, and clarity:

- **New Moon**—Time to set intentions, rest, and reset. The seed moment. Plant new ideas, but don't expect immediate growth.

- **Waxing Crescent**—Begin new projects with gentle energy. Take the first small steps toward your new moon intentions.

- **First Quarter**—Take bold action. Overcome resistance. This is when you meet the first challenges and push through.

- **Waxing Gibbous**—Adjust, refine, and prepare for results. Fine-tune your approach as momentum builds.

- **Full Moon**—Peak energy, clarity, emotional intensity. Harvest time. Maximum visibility and manifestation power.

- **Waning Gibbous**—Reflect, share, express insights. This is the integration phase. Share what you've learned.

- **Last Quarter**—Release what's no longer working. Clear out the old to make space for the new.

- **Waning Crescent**—Deep rest, closure, inner work. Preparation for the next cycle. Sacred pause.

Frequency Intelligence uses your personal moon transits to show how each phase affects you specifically based on your natal chart. Your Moon sign, house placement, and current transits all influence how lunar energy moves through your system.

These cycles help determine the energetic theme you're in at any given time:

Personal Year (1–9): The Overarching Lesson and Theme of Your Current Year

 new beginnings, independence, fresh starts

 partnership, cooperation, patience

 creative expression, social expansion

 building, structure, hard work

 freedom, change, adventure

 responsibility, family, service

 inner work, spirituality, reflection

 material achievement, power, recognition

 endings, completion, release

Personal Month: monthly theme within the year (e.g., action versus reflection)

Personal Day: micro-cycle guidance, perfect for day-to-day flow planning

Example: A Personal Year 1 = fresh start. A Personal Month 9 = release. A Personal Day 4 = structure and systems.

3. Personal Energy Seasons—Bio and Emotional Rhythm

This is your custom rhythm, put into action from your inputs and wearable data. Over time, Frequency Intelligence learns when:

- You naturally experience energy highs and lows.

- Your focus is sharper or more distracted.

- Your mood is most stable or volatile.

- You're more creative than reflective.

It then overlays these patterns with cosmic and numerological data to give custom timing recommendations—from launching a business to taking a social media break.

Daily Life with the Formula

The Daily Flow Experience

Morning	Midday	Evening
Daily Frequency Briefing: Wake up to your energy zone, mood code, and personalized mantra	Real-Time Adjustment: Receive alerts if stress level spikes or energy level drops.	Reflection and Regeneration Tools: Close with a sound frequency or guided journaling session.

Energy Zone of the Day

You're told whether your core elemental energy today is:

- **Fire**—Act, initiate, create

- **Earth**—Build, structure, ground

- **Air**—Communicate, connect, think

- **Water**—Restore, feel, flow

These suggestions help create daily rituals that intentionally shape your week.

The Personalized Algorithm

No two users are alike. The Formula continuously learns from your biofeedback, app engagement, and self-reporting:

- If you log a low mood for three days in a row → AI adjusts future action recommendations.

- If you ignore suggestions → The system notes your patterns and adjusts messaging style.

- If your HRV improves after specific rituals → You'll get more of those.

Result: Your app becomes a frequency mirror—a tool that reflects and refines your alignment.

The BioSync Loop

At the center of this system is what I call the BioSync Loop:

Awareness → Alignment → Action → Adjustment → Integration

It's a daily rhythm. A way of listening. A way of moving. The loop helps you calibrate—not just by what you think, but by what you feel and track.

This continuous cycle ensures you're not just following a static blueprint, but actively engaging with your energetic state as it shifts and evolves throughout your day, week, and year.

Awareness: Notice your current state (energy, mood, clarity).

Alignment: Check in with your astrological and numerological timing.

Action: Choose responses that honor your current phase. Adjustment: Track what works and what doesn't.

Integration: Begin the cycle again with sharper awareness and refined insight.

From Knowing to Living

It wasn't just the astrology insight that changed my life. It was the moment I started tracking myself.

I began journaling about my moods, dreams, irritations, energy levels, and clarity. Not just emotionally—but energetically. I started to see cycles—recurring patterns and emotional echoes.

Eventually, I created a manual version of the FQ system for my own use. I would ask daily:

- Am I in Launch, Align, or Reflect?

- What does my body want today?

- What am I forcing that doesn't want to move?

Even without an app, the effect was immediate. I stopped outsourcing clarity to mentors or trends. I started leading from alignment—not adrenaline. And the more I listened, the louder the signal became.

Real-World Examples and Case Studies

Paul—When the Blueprint Becomes a Mirror
In March 2025, I had the opportunity to test the Frequency Intelligence system with Paul, a colleague who had been experiencing a particular kind of professional restlessness that conventional approaches hadn't been able to address.

Paul wasn't unhappy with his career, nor was he burned out in any obvious way. His work performance was strong, his leadership was respected, and from external measures, everything appeared to be

66

functioning well. Yet he carried an invisible weight—a sense that something fundamental was misaligned.

He described feeling mentally overloaded but emotionally flat, restless without a clear cause, and irritated by a persistent sense that he was operating at cross-purposes with his own nature. We had explored traditional solutions, including executive coaching, leadership development programs, and performance optimization strategies. Nothing quite addressed the core issue.

When I offered to create his Frequency Blueprint, he agreed with the measured skepticism of someone trained in analytical thinking who nonetheless recognized that conventional approaches had reached their limits.

I generated his complete blueprint analysis and presented it to him without extensive explanation or interpretation. The document spoke for itself—a comprehensive mapping of his energetic patterns, natural rhythms, and the specific ways his system processed stress, creativity, and decision-making.

What happened next was subtle but unmistakable. I watched Paul's energy shift as he read, a quiet recognition crossing his features. The restlessness he couldn't articulate had suddenly been given language. The internal conflicts he couldn't explain were reflected back to him not as problems to be solved, but as aspects of his natural design that had been misunderstood or suppressed.

Paul processes information internally and deliberately. He doesn't make dramatic shifts or sudden announcements. However, from that point forward, there was a noticeable lightening in his presence, a settling that suggested something had clicked into place at a fundamental level.

Several weeks later, he shared his perspective: "It wasn't that I was dissatisfied with my work or my life. The feelings seemed to come from somewhere else, some other time, and they kept interfering with my ability to be present with what was actually happening."

This observation captures something essential about how Frequency Intelligence functions. It helps individuals trace energetic static to its source, distinguishing between current circumstances and inherited patterns, outdated conditioning, or misalignment with natural rhythms that create persistent background interference.

The blueprint didn't fix Paul—it revealed him. It provided language for patterns he had always sensed but never been able to articulate, and perhaps most importantly, it gave him permission to trust his own energetic intelligence rather than continuing to override it with purely logical analysis.

Sometimes the most profound transformations happen not through dramatic intervention, but through accurate recognition. Paul's case demonstrates that individuals aren't broken when they feel inexplicably off-center despite external success—they're often simply operating out of sync with their soul-level energetic design.

Case Study: Emma, the Burnt-Out CEO

The Problem: Emma was experiencing constant fatigue despite getting adequate sleep and rest. She was pushing through daily tasks but felt increasingly disconnected from her work.

The Analysis: The AI revealed she was in Personal Year 9 (completion cycle) with Moon opposition Mars transit, indicating a deep clearing phase.

The Recommendation: "You are in a deep clearing phase. Stop trying to build. Release, grieve, finish old projects."

The Result: After ten days of following energy rhythms and using frequency rituals, Emma regained clarity and felt reconnected to her purpose.

Case Study: Daniel, the Overthinker

The Problem: Daniel's HRV was dropping every day around midday during work hours, leading to decision paralysis and mental fog.

The Analysis: The system showed Mercury square Uranus transit, combined with his mental biorhythm being in a low phase.

The Solution: Fifteen-minute binaural beat sessions combined with specific breathwork exercises during his energy dips.

The Result: HRV stabilized, energy reset, and focus restored within the same day.

A Day in the Life: Sophia's User Flow

Let's imagine Sophia, a user who has synced her biometric wearable to the Frequency Intelligence platform and has entered her precise birth data. Here's how her day looks, shaped by the Quantum Frequency Formula:

7:00 a.m.—Wake-Up Sync. Sophia opens the Frequency Intelligence app and receives her Daily Energetic Briefing:

- Today's Frequency Score: 84/100 (high alignment).

- Primary Energy Zone: Fire (driven, assertive).

- Planetary Influences: Mars trine Sun. Take bold action.

- Numerology Insight: Personal Day 1—Great for new beginnings.

- Biofeedback: Slight drop in HRV suggests mild stress—recommended: five-minute calming breathwork.

- Suggested Focus: Launch or take action on new ideas.

10:00 a.m.—Energy Alert. As she heads into a morning meeting, her wearable detects an energy dip. Notification: "Your HRV has dropped—Neptune square Moon is increasing emotional sensitivity. Pause before reacting. Suggested mantra: I flow with clarity."

Sophia opens the app. She takes three minutes to recalibrate with a light frequency from the wearable and a short guided breathwork session synced with her zodiac profile.

1:30 p.m.—Optimization Pulse. At lunch, Sophia opens the "Optimize" tab.

- Energy Zone: Stable.

- Planetary Shift Alert: Moon is void-of-course—best for routine tasks.

- Personal Tip: "Avoid signing contracts this afternoon. Use this time to organize and plan."

She reschedules her legal call and instead journals about her business vision.

8:00 p.m.—Evening Reflection. Before bed, Sophia does a quick check-in. She logs her mood, and the AI reflects back: "Today was an 84 percent alignment day. Your decisions were mostly in sync. Continue this momentum tomorrow—another high-frequency day is coming."

Her wearable glows blue, indicating a calm energy field. The system suggests a calming sound frequency to support deep sleep, which aligns with her Moon sign in Cancer.

From reactive to aligned living: What once felt chaotic is now structured and aligned. Sophia is no longer guessing when to push and when to rest. She lives with her cycles—not against them.

Feminine Flow vs. Masculine Productivity

This is not about gender. It's about energy.

Masculine energy: linear, structured, goal-focused—do, go, produce

Feminine energy: cyclical, intuitive, receptive—feel, sense, trust

Most of us—especially high achievers—are conditioned to embody masculine energy. We value productivity. We chase results. We plan every hour.

However, feminine flow doesn't move in straight lines. It moves in spirals.

When you override your flow, you override your genius.

Feminine intelligence teaches you to:

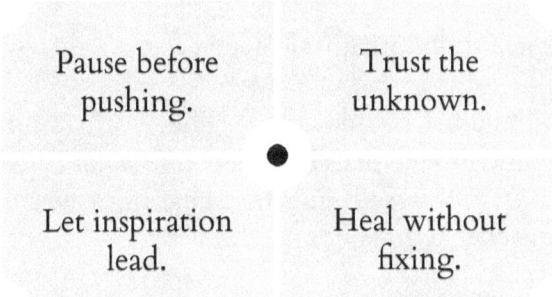

Pause before pushing.

Trust the unknown.

Let inspiration lead.

Heal without fixing.

My most significant leadership shift was learning to feel safe in the pause. That is power.

Embodied Flow: What Each Zone Feels Like

You don't have to think your way into your zone. You can feel it.

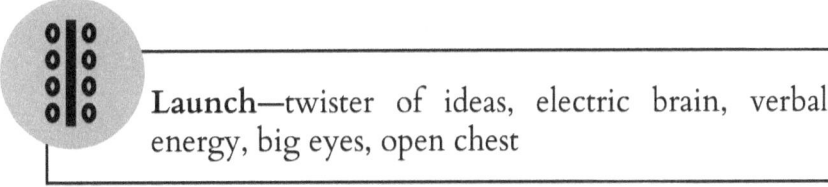

Launch—twister of ideas, electric brain, verbal energy, big eyes, open chest

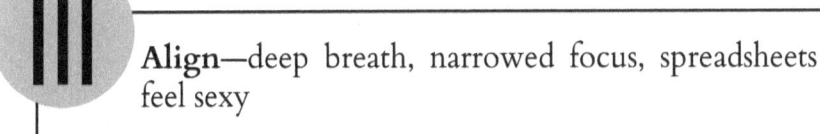

Align—deep breath, narrowed focus, spreadsheets feel sexy

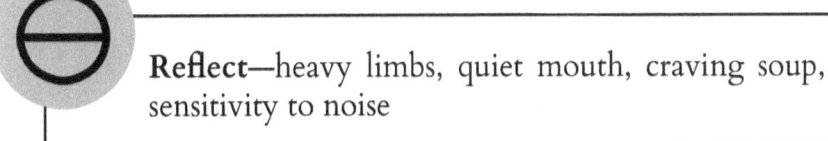

Reflect—heavy limbs, quiet mouth, craving soup, sensitivity to noise

Once you know how each zone lives in your body, you'll stop guessing. You'll start sensing.

I've wanted to write a book for years, but I've never been able to start. I overplanned. I felt resistance—until this one arrived.

I didn't force it. I didn't plan it. I received it.

And once it landed, I couldn't stop. The words poured through me. My husband joked that I looked like a teenager playing a video game. I was obsessed—not in a chaotic way, but in a clear, joyful, focused way.

That's Launch. That's alignment—the right message in the right season.

What People Get Wrong About Astrology and AI

Most people think astrology is mystical and ungrounded. They believe AI is cold and clinical. Yet when you merge them, something extraordinary happens: you give logic a soul—and you give intuition a voice.

You are not one or the other. You are both. Your body and your spirit. Your data and your dreams. This system reflects that back to you.

This is the kind of intelligence we're reclaiming: subtle, elegant, energizing. Not adrenaline—but clarity. Not chaos—but coherence.

One Time I Didn't Listen

In late 2023, I was planning a business investment. The logic made sense. The money was good. Yet everything in my body said no. I delayed the deal, trying to wait out Mercury Retrograde—but I signed in the shadow phase.

It was a disaster: delays, miscommunications, lost time. Not because the idea was wrong—but because the timing was.

That moment taught me something vital: Your blueprint always speaks. The question is—are you listening?

The truth is, I often notice when things go wrong more than when they go right. It's in the tension, the resistance, the procrastination that my misalignment becomes loud. Although when I'm aligned, the energy feels... light, clear, sustainable. Not euphoric. Just right. That's the energy I want you to feel. Not hype. Not hustle. Just resonance.

Scientific and Spiritual Foundations

This system is not pseudoscience—it's pattern intelligence, rooted in both ancient wisdom and current science.

The Science Behind the System

Heart Rate Variability (HRV) is one of the most accurate predictors of resilience and nervous system balance. HRV measures the variation in time between heartbeats, indicating how well your autonomic nervous system adapts to stress and recovery.

Chronobiology shows how body rhythms are time-sensitive. Our circadian rhythms, ultradian cycles, and seasonal patterns all influence our optimal performance windows.

Astrocyclic Theory (used in financial astrology) demonstrates correlations between planetary movements and macroeconomic cycles. If markets respond to cosmic timing, why wouldn't human energy systems?

Jungian Psychology supports archetypal patterns aligned with astrological symbolism. Carl Jung himself studied astrology and saw natal charts as maps of the unconscious psyche.

What makes Frequency Intelligence unique is its integration of multiple valid systems:

- Astrological timing has been used for millennia to guide human decisions.

- Numerological cycles appear across cultures as vibrational organizing principles.

- Biorhythm tracking shows measurable patterns in human energy.

- AI pattern recognition can identify subtle correlations humans might miss.

This isn't about belief—it's about pattern recognition and practical application.

Practical Integration Tools

Manual Frequency Check-In

You don't need the entire app to begin. Start here:

1. Get your signature natal chart online (date, time, place of birth). Try astro.com or any free tool.

2. Track your mood, body, focus, and emotions for one week.

3. Each morning, ask:

   - How does my body feel?

   - Where am I in my energy today: Launch, Align, Reflect?

   - What would feel good—not just productive?

You're already intuitive. This system merely gives your intuition structure.

Each day, open your journal and ask:

- What's present in my body right now?

- Do I feel expansion (Launch), structure (Align), or withdrawal (Reflect)?

- If I trusted this fully, what would I choose today?

Advanced Integration Practice
Here's how to tune into your blueprint:

1. Get your 360° natal chart (date, time, place of birth).

2. Identify your Sun, Moon, and Rising signs.

3. Track your mood, energy, and clarity in a journal for three weeks.

4. Begin to notice patterns. Noticing is the beginning of mastery.

Your energy body speaks in patterns. The more you listen, the more precise your life becomes.

Flow Mantra

Not every season is a harvest. Some are soil. Some are seed.

You are not lazy for resting. You are not better for launching.

You are whole when you listen.

Business and Leadership Applications

Flow Mapping at Scale (Teams, Families, Leadership)
The Flow Map isn't just personal. It can transform how we work and lead.

In families:
- One child may be in Launch—ready to socialize.
- Another may be in Reflect—needing quiet.
- You adjust intuitively.

In teams:
- Before a product launch, you check the team's Flow Map.
- Three are in Align—perfect for planning.
- One is in Reflect—better to reschedule their task.

In leadership:
- You schedule tough conversations in Launch.
- You use Align weeks for strategy.
- You take Reflect days to review, refine, and restore.

This is how we build resilient, human, frequency-led systems.

Energetic Leadership

Imagine onboarding your entire company with Frequency Intelligence:

- Each person receives their blueprint.
- Leaders schedule sprints based on team-wide Launch Zones.
- HR aligns reviews and hiring with peak clarity cycles.
- Employees take aligned rest—not just vacation days.

Work becomes intelligent. Rhythm replaces burnout. Alignment replaces force.

When people first begin working with their Frequency Blueprint, one of the most surprising realizations is where they've been overriding it unconsciously.

These "energetic blind spots" might look like:

- Always launching during misaligned timing

- Assuming rest is laziness

- Ignoring intuition when logic appears more reliable

- Needing breakdowns before allowing breakthroughs

Common Signs You're Ignoring Your Frequency:

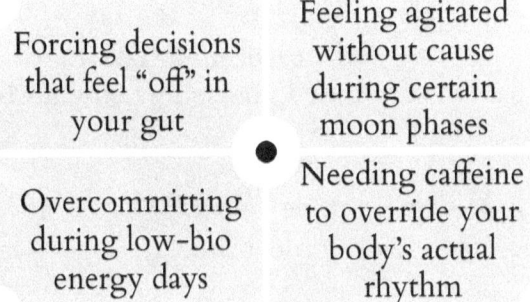

Forcing decisions that feel "off" in your gut

Feeling agitated without cause during certain moon phases

Overcommitting during low-bio energy days

Needing caffeine to override your body's actual rhythm

These are not failures. They're flags. Signals that your blueprint is asking to be honored.

By becoming conscious of these patterns, you begin to shift. You catch yourself earlier. You choose differently. You reclaim power in the smallest, most practical ways.

Case Study: Reflecting Too Late

In June 2023, I decided to take a step back from work. I ended contracts. I thought I needed space, but I was in the wrong energy when I made the decision.

I was emotional. I was in Reflect, but I treated it like Launch.

What happened?

Income slowed.

My business lost momentum.

I felt worse, not better.

It wasn't rest. It was a misaligned reaction.

If I had paused, journaled, waited three days—I would have seen the pattern. That's the cost of misreading your zone.

Why Most People Are Operating Out of Sync

Have you ever launched something at the wrong time? Spoken up when no one was ready to hear it? Felt foggy in a season that required clarity—or pushed yourself when your body begged for rest?

It's not because you lacked drive, talent, or vision. It's because you didn't yet have access to your blueprint.

Modern culture teaches us to move in straight lines: wake up, work hard, stay consistent, repeat. In reality, humans are not linear. We are cyclical. Our energy moves in waves—physical, emotional, mental, spiritual.

When we ignore these waves, we experience friction. We call it burnout, confusion, low energy, and creative blocks, but it's not a pathology. It's misalignment.

The Frequency Blueprint shows you how to move with your energy—not against it. It reveals the optimal rhythm for your life, and it's different for everyone.

We each have different planetary placements. Different numerology codes. Different energetic signatures.

What energizes one person might exhaust another. What feels like success for you might look completely different for someone else. Understanding your Frequency Blueprint means finally letting go of the myth of sameness. It means leading from sovereignty, not standardization.

What the Blueprint Does

The Frequency Blueprint doesn't tell you what to do. It tells you when to do it—and how to stay aligned while doing it.

Most people run on someone else's schedule. They follow deadlines instead of inner data. They burn out, push through, and build lives that appear successful on paper but ultimately collapse within.

Frequency Intelligence changes that.

You no longer need to guess when to launch, rest, initiate, or retreat. You have a system for your own rhythm.

Imagine your OS—your operating system—not just predicting your peak focus window, but syncing it with planetary flow and numerological timing. That's energetic precision.

A System of Alignment, Not Control

This is not a system for predicting your future. It's a tool for radical self-alignment.

The Frequency Blueprint does not tell you what to do. It tells you when to do it and how to do it in a way that aligns with your current energetic climate.

It's about syncing your outer actions with your inner wisdom and cosmic timing. It's about designing your day, your work, your habits—your life—from the inside out.

You may already know your Sun sign. Maybe even your Rising sign. However, very few people know how to live by their chart.

The Frequency Blueprint gives you real-time guidance by combining timeless systems (astrology, numerology) with modern tools (AI, mood tracking, biofeedback). This makes it actionable, dynamic, and tailored to your actual life, not generic advice.

Ultimately, that's the key.

Generic astrology gives you identity. Frequency Intelligence gives you strategy.

Unlike static personality tests or astrology apps, Frequency Intelligence combines real-time physiological feedback with predictive timing logic, delivering personalized, dynamic, and actionable insights in fast-moving environments.

This Is What FQ Actually Gives You

It's not just another tool. It's a framework for remembering.

It teaches you to:

- Feel the difference between forcing and flowing.

- Catch energetic dissonance before it turns into burnout.

- Navigate timing not from urgency, but inner knowing.

- Discern intuition from fear, pressure, or performance.

- Move when it's true—not just when it's trending.

Living by Your Frequency Blueprint

Once you begin living by your blueprint, life stops feeling like guesswork.

You begin to:

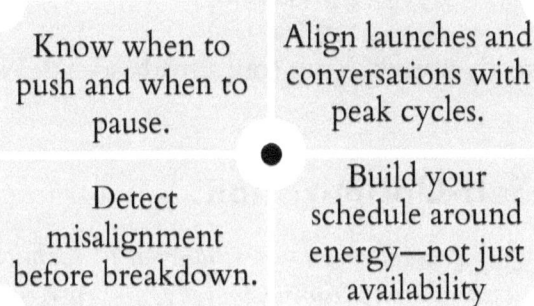

Know when to push and when to pause.

Align launches and conversations with peak cycles.

Detect misalignment before breakdown.

Build your schedule around energy—not just availability

You stop chasing someone else's path—and start walking your own.

That's Frequency Intelligence, and it starts here.

Mini Activation: Are You in Sync Right Now?
Before moving on, pause and scan your body.

Are you energized or exhausted? Clear or foggy? Open or resistant? Now look at your calendar. Are you in a Launch zone but scheduling high-stress output? Are you in a Reflect zone but forcing decisions?

Just this awareness is a win. The goal of Frequency Intelligence isn't to be perfect—it's to be precise.

You Don't Have to Earn Your Rhythm

This chapter is not here to impress you. It's here to remind you.

You already have a rhythm. You already have a blueprint, and it has been guiding you long before you had words for it.

What FQ offers is not a new identity. It's a new intimacy—with yourself, your timing, your truth.

Because in a world that moves too fast and talks too loud, the most advanced form of intelligence is not speed. It's sovereignty.

You don't need more motivation. You need truth. You don't need more willpower. You need to remember your wave.

Your body already knows. Your soul already speaks. Now it's time to listen.

The New Self-Optimization

Imagine waking up every day not guessing what to do, but being guided into alignment with your best timing, biology, and energy.

You don't need to force anymore. You need to listen. You don't need to hustle harder. You need to vibrate smarter.

This is not the age of hustle. This is the age of frequency. So if you're reading this book, it means you're ready to tune in.

Most people treat energy like a battery: charge, spend, repeat. In contrast, your Frequency Blueprint isn't a battery. It's a loop.

When you honor each part—Launch, Align, Reflect—your rhythm becomes regenerative. You're no longer surviving off your energy. You're circulating it.

Metaphors to Anchor the Map

Still confused? Try these metaphors:

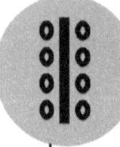 **Launch**—Spring / Sunrise / Exhale / Creative spark

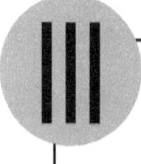 **Align**—Summer / Noon / Focused breath / Structural editing

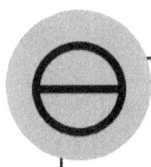

> **Reflect**—Winter / Moonlight / Inhale / Energetic composting

Or think of it like farming:

- **Launch** = Plant the seed.

- **Align** = Tend the soil.

- **Reflect** = Let it rest before harvesting.

Flow Is a Lifestyle, Not a Hack

You begin noticing your personal cues:

- Clarity on Day 3s.

- Overwhelm during First Quarter Moons.

- Your nervous system becomes more open during Air-sign transits.

These aren't accidents. They're your energetic fingerprint. The more you track, the more you trust.

Living by the Flow Map isn't a productivity hack. It's a lifestyle redesign.

It's not "How do I get more done with less effort?" Instead, it's "How do I stop betraying my timing?"

You don't grow a rose faster by yelling at it. You give it sun, water, space, and time. You are the same.

Chapter Integration Ritual *Frequency Anchor*

Close your eyes. Take a breath. Ask yourself this: Where am I in my flow today?

If your body says rest, rest. If your mind says reflect, reflect. If your heart says go, then go.

You are the technology. Frequency Intelligence only helps you remember.

There's a pattern pulsing beneath every decision you've ever made.

You may not always see it, but you've felt it.

It's in the mornings when everything flows effortlessly. The days when your timing is cosmic. The seasons when, no matter how hard you try, nothing seems to land.

That invisible pattern? It's your Frequency Blueprint, and it's been guiding you all along.

In practice, most of us were never taught to read it. We were handed calendars and deadlines, clocks and goals. We were conditioned to value performance over presence, strategy over stillness, progress over timing.

We learned how to act but not how to align.

This chapter is the beginning of a new relationship with your own energy—one where your timing is no longer an accident. Where your success doesn't cost you your nervous system, your intuition becomes data, and your decisions become aligned by design.

You weren't born to blend in. You were born to broadcast.

Integration: Daily Flow Tracker (Optional Practice)

Want to try this? Create a journal with these prompts:

- Morning check-in: What zone am I in? Why?

- Midday shift: Did it change?

- Evening reflection: What worked? What didn't?
- Think of one word for tomorrow's desired zone.

After a week, you'll start to see your patterns, and those patterns are gold.

What Changed My Business Forever

In early January 2025, I was offered 14 million DKK in funding to scale ReyRey. A dream moment. A financial threshold most founders crave.

Nevertheless, everything in my body said no. Not from fear. From clarity.

It was one of the toughest decisions I've ever made. For weeks, I spiraled. I doubted myself. I questioned whether I had sabotaged something sacred.

Yet, just weeks later, in late February, the idea for Frequency Intelligence arrived. Not from strategy. From silence. A download. A pulse. An embodied system that felt like it had been waiting for me to clear space.

That clarity? It wasn't a surprise. It was what my astrologer had told me back in April 2023: "You're going to build something no one else can name yet. It will arrive suddenly—if your timing is right."

He passed away later that year. Regardless, every time I work on this book, speak this system, or teach this rhythm, I feel his voice beside mine. He didn't just see my path. He named it.

You Are the Technology

This isn't a personality tool. This is Frequency Intelligence—an integration of logic and spirit, intuition and science.

You're not outsourcing your power to a system. You're reclaiming it.

This blueprint is your permission to stop performing and start aligning. It's a mirror for what your body already knows. A system that tells you, "You didn't miss your moment. You were becoming it."

The Three-Layer Quantum Engine

At the heart of the Quantum Frequency Formula lies what I call the Three-Layer Quantum Engine—a sophisticated AI architecture that processes your multidimensional data into precise, actionable guidance. This engine operates on three distinct but interconnected layers, each serving a specific function in translating your energetic state into practical wisdom.

Layer 1: The Alignment Layer—When You're Energetically "Open"

The Alignment Layer detects windows where your body, mind, and cosmic energy are in harmony. These are your optimal days for high-impact activities that require your full energetic presence.

What it tracks:
- HRV feedback above your personal baseline

- Favorable planetary transits to your natal chart

- Personal numerology days that support action (1, 3, 5, 8)

- Emotional stability indicators from your mood logs

- Physical energy peaks from your movement and sleep data

Optimal activities during Alignment:
- Launching new projects or products

- Important presentations or pitches

- Difficult conversations or negotiations

- Travel or major transitions

- Manifesting and visioning work

Think of these as your green-light signals. When the Alignment Layer is active, the system might tell you, "Today's configuration supports bold moves. Your HRV is optimal, Mars is trine your Midheaven, and you're in a Personal Day 1. This is your window."

Layer 2: The Resistance Layer – When to Pause or Reflect

The Resistance Layer picks up energetic friction fields—periods when pushing forward would create more struggle than flow. These aren't "bad" days; they're recalibration periods that serve essential functions in your growth cycle.

What it detects:
- HRV drops below your threshold

- Challenging planetary aspects (squares, oppositions)

- Personal numerology cycles that call for introspection (7, 9)

- Emotional volatility patterns

- Physical depletion markers

Best Activities During Resistance:
- Journaling and inner work

- Healing practices and therapy

- Letting go of what's no longer serving

- Saying "no" to opportunities

- Rest and regeneration

The Resistance Layer might advise this: "Mercury is square your natal Moon while your HRV shows stress. Your emotional rhythm is in a low phase. Today is for processing, not pushing. Honor the pause."

The Optimization Layer is the most sophisticated component. It takes the data from the first two layers and creates personalized protocols to either amplify your alignment or support you through resistance.

During Alignment periods, it suggests:

- Specific morning rituals to enhance your natural flow

- Optimal timing for prioritized activities

- Astro-based affirmations matched to current transits

- Sound frequencies that amplify your energy signature

- Movement practices that support your current state

During Resistance periods, it offers:

- Gentle healing modalities (meditation, breathwork)

- Protective energy practices

- Emotional release techniques

- Sound healing frequencies for nervous system regulation

- Restorative activities aligned with your astrological makeup

Example optimization sequence: "You're entering a three-day Alignment window. Begin each morning with ten minutes of 528 Hz frequency meditation. Your Sagittarius Rising thrives with movement—take a walk before high-priority calls. Use the affirmation: 'I trust my vision and act with clarity.' Avoid decision-making after 6 p.m. when the Moon squares your Mercury."

Over time, the Optimization Layer learns what works specifically for you. If certain frequency combinations improve your HRV, you'll receive more of those. If specific rituals correlate with better decision-making, they'll be prioritized in your daily recommendations.

The Four Energy Bodies and Frequency Integration

Your Frequency Blueprint operates through four distinct yet interconnected energy bodies. Understanding how each body responds to different frequencies allows you to calibrate your entire system for precision.

The Physical Energy Body

Your physical energy body encompasses your biological rhythms, nervous system regulation, and embodied vitality. This body responds most directly to:

Frequency Interventions:

- 174 Hz—pain relief and muscle tension release
- 285 Hz—cellular healing and tissue regeneration
- 396 Hz—root chakra grounding and physical stability
- Red light therapy (660-850 nm)—cellular energy production
- Breathwork patterns—matched to your current HRV state

Signs of Physical Body Misalignment:

- Chronic fatigue despite adequate sleep
- Persistent muscle tension or pain
- Digestive issues or appetite changes
- Sleep disruption or circadian rhythm dysfunction
- Frequent illness or lowered immunity

Physical Body Optimization Through the Blueprint:

When your chart indicates Mars transits or you're in a high-energy numerology cycle—but your physical body shows signs of depletion—the system initiates a bridge protocol. Instead of pushing through, you might receive, "Your spirit is ready to launch, but your body needs support. Try fifteen minutes of 285 Hz frequency therapy while doing gentle movement. Honor both energies."

The Emotional Energy Body

Your emotional energy body processes feelings, relationships, and creative expression. It's highly sensitive to lunar cycles and water element transits.

Frequency Interventions:

- 417 Hz—emotional release and trauma healing
- 528 Hz—love frequency for heart opening
- 639 Hz—relationship harmony and communication
- Blue light therapy—emotional regulation
- Specific breathwork—emotional processing (4-7-8 breathing, box breathing)

Signs of Emotional Body Misalignment:

- Mood swings that seem unrelated to external circumstances
- Difficulty accessing or expressing emotions
- Relationship conflicts or communication breakdowns
- Creative blocks or loss of inspiration
- Feeling emotionally "numb" or overwhelmed

Emotional Body Attunement:

During challenging emotional transits (like Moon opposite your natal Venus), the system might recommend, "Your emotional body is processing relationship patterns. Use 417 Hz frequency while journaling about what you're releasing. This is healing work, not dysfunction."

The Mental Energy Body

Your mental energy body governs thought patterns, decision-making, and information processing. This body responds strongly to Mercury transits and air element activations.

Frequency Interventions:

- 741 Hz—mental clarity and problem-solving

- 852 Hz—intuitive insight and mental flexibility

- 963 Hz—higher consciousness and spiritual thinking

- Binaural beats in gamma range (40 Hz)—focus

- Nootropic breathing patterns—cognitive enhancement

Signs of Mental Body Misalignment:

- Brain fog or difficulty concentrating

- Overthinking or mental loops

- Poor decision-making or analysis paralysis

- Memory issues or learning difficulties

- Scattered thinking or inability to prioritize

Mental Body Optimization:

When Mercury is retrograde, but you need mental clarity for important decisions, the system creates cognitive support protocols: "Mercury retrograde is affecting your mental body. Use a 741 Hz frequency for twenty minutes before the meeting. Practice single-tasking today. Trust your prepared materials over spontaneous thinking."

The Spiritual Energy Body

Your spiritual energy body connects you to purpose, meaning, and transcendent awareness. Planet transits and spiritual practices activate this body.

Frequency Interventions:

- 963 Hz—pineal gland activation and spiritual connection
- 1111 Hz—cellular awakening and DNA activation
- 40 Hz gamma waves—mystical experience and unity consciousness
- Tibetan singing bowls—tuned to planetary frequencies
- Contemplative practices—aligned with your natal chart

Signs of Spiritual Body Misalignment:

- Loss of meaning or purpose
- Disconnection from intuitive guidance
- Spiritual bypassing or materialism
- Inability to access flow states
- Feeling separate from something larger

Spiritual Body Activation:

During significant spiritual transits (like Jupiter trine your natal Neptune), the system supports deeper connection: "Your spiritual body is ready for expansion. Use 963 Hz meditation at sunrise. Your Pisces Moon is activated—trust your visions and dreams. This is a portal for spiritual growth."

Integration Practice: Four-Body Scan

Here's a daily practice to attune to all four energy bodies:

Morning Four-Body Check-In:

Physical:	Emotional:
Scan from head to toe. Where do you feel energy, tension, or aliveness?	What feelings are present? What wants to be expressed?

Mental:	Spiritual:
How clear or foggy is your thinking? What thoughts are dominant?	Do you feel connected to something larger? What's your sense of purpose today?

Based on this scan, choose frequencies and practices that support your current state across all four bodies.

Advanced Frequency Healing Integration

Planetary Frequency Correspondences

Each planet in your chart resonates with specific frequencies that can be used for targeted healing and enhancement:

- **Sun (Core Identity):** 126.22 Hz—confidence, vitality, leadership

- **Moon (Emotions):** 210.42 Hz—intuition, nurturing, emotional flow

- **Mercury (Communication):** 141.27 Hz—mental clarity, learning, expression

- **Venus (Love/Creativity):** 221.23 Hz—relationships, beauty, artistic flow

- **Mars (Action/Drive):** 144.72 Hz—motivation, courage, physical energy

- **Jupiter (Expansion):** 183.58 Hz—abundance, wisdom, growth

- **Saturn (Structure):** 147.85 Hz—discipline, boundaries, mastery

Personalized Sound Healing Protocols

Based on your natal chart and current transits, Frequency Intelligence creates custom sound healing sessions:

Example: Mars Return Protocol

During your Mars return (every two years), when Mars returns to its natal position:

- Presession: 396 Hz grounding for five minutes

- Main session: 144.72 Hz (Mars frequency) for twenty minutes

- Integration: 528 Hz heart opening for ten minutes

- Closing: silence and intention setting

Example: Mercury Retrograde Support

During Mercury retrograde periods:

- Morning: 741 Hz for mental clarity before priority communications

- Midday: 417 Hz if miscommunications arise

- Evening: 852 Hz for intuitive problem-solving

Different combinations of binaural beats can induce specific consciousness states aligned with your current needs:

Focus and Productivity—Align Zone:
- Base frequency: 40 Hz (gamma wave)

- Binaural beat: 14 Hz difference

- Duration: 25-45 minutes

- Best during: Mercury direct periods, Personal Day 4 or 8

Creative Flow (Launch Zone):
- Base frequency: 10 Hz (alpha wave)

- Binaural beat: 6 Hz difference

- Duration: 30-60 minutes

- Best during: Venus or Jupiter transits, Personal Day 3 or 5

Deep Rest and Integration—Reflect Zone:
- Base frequency: 4 Hz (theta wave)

- Binaural beat: 2 Hz difference

- Duration: 20-40 minutes

- Best during: Moon in water signs, Personal Days 7 or 9

Seasonal Energy Cycles and Annual Frequency Mapping

Your Frequency Blueprint shifts throughout the year, influenced by both cosmic cycles and natural seasonal rhythms. Understanding these patterns allows for long-term energy planning.

Spring Equinox to Summer Solstice—Launch Season

- Dominant energy: cardinal fire and earth

- Optimal for: new beginnings, planting seeds, external action

- Frequency support: higher Hz ranges (528-963 Hz) for activation

- Planetary focus: Sun, Mars, Jupiter transits

- Numerology emphasis: Personal Years 1, 3, 8

Summer Solstice to Fall Equinox—Align Season

- Dominant energy: fixed fire and mutable earth

- Optimal for: building momentum, sustained effort, refinement

- Frequency support: mid-range Hz (417-741 Hz) for stability

- Planetary focus: Venus, Mercury, Saturn transits

- Numerology emphasis: Personal Years 4, 6

Fall Equinox to Winter Solstice—Harvest/Reflect Season

- Dominant energy: cardinal air and mutable water

- Optimal for: completion, release, inner work

- Frequency support: lower Hz ranges (174-396 Hz) for grounding

- Planetary focus: Moon, Neptune, Pluto transits

Numerology emphasis: Personal Years 7, 9

Winter Solstice to Spring Equinox—Deep Reflect Season

- Dominant energy: cardinal earth and fixed water

- Optimal for: rest, visioning, spiritual connection

- Frequency support: very low Hz and silence for regeneration

- Planetary focus: Saturn, Uranus, inner work transits

- Numerology emphasis: Personal Year 7, master numbers

Your Personal Seasonal Pattern

Beyond the universal seasonal cycle, your individual chart creates a personal seasonal pattern based on:

- Solar return (birthday) as your personal new year

- Lunar return (every 28 days) as a monthly renewal

- Planetary returns (Mercury every 88 days, Venus every 225 days, Mars every 2 years)

- Progressed chart shifts that create multi-year themes

Example: Personal Seasonal Map—If you're a Scorpio Sun with Gemini Rising:

- **Personal Spring:** Scorpio season (late October– late November)—a more primal transformation and regeneration

- **Personal Summer:** Aquarius season (late January–late February)—innovation and community building

- **Personal Fall:** Gemini season (late May–late June)— communication and learning integration

- **Personal Winter:** Virgo season (late August–late September)—practical implementation and refinement

Cultural and Ancestral Frequency Patterns

Your Frequency Blueprint is influenced not only by cosmic timing but also by ancestral and cultural energetic patterns passed down through family lineages.

Inherited Patterns:

- Family trauma stored in your nervous system

- Generational success or struggle patterns

- Cultural relationship to money, work, and spirituality

- Ancestral gifts and talents that emerge at certain life phases

Astrological Inheritance: Research shows that children often carry prominent placements from their parents' or grandparents' charts:

- Similar Sun, Moon, or Rising signs across generations

- Repeated planetary aspects (Venus trine Jupiter spanning family lines)

- Shared difficult transits that activate family healing themes

Frequency Healing for Ancestral Patterns: When your blueprint shows ancestral activation (often during Saturn returns, Pluto transits, or family-related eclipses):

- 174 Hz for releasing inherited trauma

- 528 Hz for healing family relationship patterns

- 741 Hz for breaking unconscious family programming

- 963 Hz for connecting with ancestral wisdom rather than wounds

Your cultural background creates specific resonance patterns: Northern European lineages often resonate with:

- Earth element frequencies during winter months

- Solar frequencies during brief summers

- Structured, disciplined frequency patterns

Mediterranean lineages often resonate with:

- Fire element frequencies year-round

- Social and communal frequency patterns

- Passionate, expressive energy signatures

East Asian lineages often resonate with:

- Balanced, harmonious frequency combinations

- Seasonal attunement and natural rhythm honoring

- Contemplative and meditative frequency practices

Indigenous lineages often resonate with:

- Drum and earth-based frequencies

- Lunar and seasonal cycle attunement

- Community and land-based frequency practices

Family Blueprint Integration

Practice: Family Energy Mapping

1. Gather birth data for parents and grandparents, if available.

2. Look for patterns, such as repeated signs, aspects, and house placements.

3. Identify family themes: What challenges repeat? What gifts are passed down?

4. Create healing frequencies: Use planetary frequencies to heal family patterns while honoring family gifts.

Example: Family Healing Session: If your family has a pattern of Saturn in Capricorn (control, workaholism, emotional restriction):

- Opening: 174 Hz to release inherited tension

- Healing: 147.85 Hz (Saturn frequency) to transform the pattern

- Integration: 528 Hz to bring love to the family lineage

- Closing: gratitude for family gifts while releasing family limitations

Advanced Troubleshooting *When the System Doesn't Work*

Even the most sophisticated system sometimes fails to align with your lived experience. Here's how to troubleshoot common discrepancies and refine your blueprint.

Common Misalignment Scenarios

Scenario 1: The System Says Launch, but You Feel Resistant

- Possible causes: You may be experiencing unprocessed emotions from the previous cycle, physical depletion, or environmental stress.

- Investigation: Check your four energy bodies individually.

- Solution: Honor the resistance first, then gentle movement toward launch energy.

Scenario 2: You're in Reflect, but External Demands Require Action

- Possible causes: Life circumstances don't align with natural rhythm.

- Investigation: Find micro-moments of reflection within action requirements.

- Solution: Bring reflective quality to necessary actions—mindful execution rather than forced productivity.

- Possible causes: System hasn't learned your personal patterns yet, birth time inaccuracy, trauma affecting natural rhythm.

- Investigation: Trust your body's wisdom while gathering more data.

- Solution: Manually track for thirty days to refine the algorithm.

Advanced Calibration Techniques

Birth Time Rectification: If your blueprint feels consistently off, your birth time might be inaccurate:

- Track major life events and correlate with transits.

- Notice when planetary returns feel most activating.

- Work with an astrologer to rectify your birth time.

Trauma Integration: Past trauma can create protective patterns that override natural rhythm:

- Notice where you consistently resist blueprint guidance.

- Work with trauma-informed practitioners.

- Use frequency healing to gently restore natural flow.

Environmental Factors: Your physical environment affects frequency reception:

- EMF interference from electronics

- Geopathic stress from your location

- Seasonal affective patterns

- Urban versus natural environment impacts

Trust your body's wisdom when:

- Your intuition consistently resists guidance.

- Physical symptoms emerge when following recommendations.

- Emotional overwhelm increases rather than decreases.

- Life circumstances create safety concerns.

How to Override Mindfully:

1. Acknowledge the discrepancy: "The system says X, but I feel Y."

2. Honor both signals: Find a bridge between blueprint guidance and body wisdom.

3. Track the outcome: Note what happens when you override.

4. Refine the system: Use this data to improve future recommendations.

Team and Organizational Flow Mapping

Creating Frequency-Led Organizations

Individual Blueprint Integration:

- All team members receive personal Frequency Blueprints.

- Scheduling accommodates individual energy cycles when possible.

- Project assignments consider natural flow patterns.

Team Energy Cycles:

- Track collective team energy using aggregated data.

- Identify team Launch, Align, and Reflect periods.
- Plan major initiatives during collective high-energy phases.

Example: Marketing Team Flow Schedule

- Monday: Team energy assessment and week planning
- Tuesday–Thursday: High-focus work during the collective Align phase
- Friday: Creative brainstorming during the collective Launch phase
- Monthly: Team Reflect session for process improvement and connection

Leadership Through Frequency Intelligence

Frequency-Aware Management:

- Schedule difficult conversations during your Launch phases.
- Make major decisions during high-coherence windows.
- Take strategic retreats during Reflect cycles.
- Model energetic awareness for your team.

Meeting Optimization:

- Check team energy before important meetings.
- Adjust meeting energy to match the team's state.
- Use appropriate frequencies in meeting spaces
- Honor individual energy needs within group settings

Example: CEO Daily Rhythm

- 5:30 a.m.: Personal frequency check-in and meditation
- 6:00 a.m.: Strategic thinking during peak mental clarity

- 9:00 a.m.: Team meetings during collective high energy

- 2:00 p.m.: Creative work during natural afternoon flow

- 4:00 p.m.: Administrative tasks during declining energy

- 6:00 p.m.: Reflection and planning for the next day

Organizational Frequency Culture

Core Principles:

- Energy is a shared resource to be honored, not exploited.

- Productivity comes from alignment, not force.

- Rest is productive when it serves the natural cycle.

- Individual differences are strengths, not problems.

Implementation Strategies:

- Flexible scheduling based on individual chronotypes

- Energy-based project assignment

- Seasonal planning that honors natural cycles

- Frequency-healing spaces for restoration

The Birth Story A Template for Natural Alignment

When I gave birth to my daughter, I experienced what I now recognize as perfect frequency alignment. This experience became a template for understanding how natural flow operates in all areas of life.

The Three Phases of Birth as Flow Template

Phase 1: Launch—Early Labor

- Energy: excited anticipation, clarity of purpose

- Physical: gentle contractions, body preparing

- Mental: focused intention, present moment awareness
- Spiritual: connection to a larger process beyond personal control

Phase 2: Align—Active Labor

- Energy: intense focus, complete presence
- Physical: powerful, rhythmic contractions working in harmony
- Mental: surrendered concentration, no overthinking
- Spiritual: trust in body wisdom, letting the process lead

Phase 3: Reflect—Birth and Integration

- Energy: transcendent stillness, profound peace
- Physical: natural rest, body recovery, and bonding
- Mental: awe and integration of experience
- Spiritual: connection to the miracle of life and creation

Applying the Birth Template to Projects

Project Launch Phase: Like early labor, project launches require:

- Clear intention and vision (contractions of inspiration)
- Gentle but consistent action (early labor rhythm)
- Trust in the process rather than forcing outcomes
- Excitement balanced with patience

Project Align Phase: Like active labor, project execution needs:

- Intense focus and presence (strong contractions)
- Surrendering to the work itself rather than the ego

- Rhythmic cycles of effort and rest

- Trust in competence and preparation

Project Reflect Phase: Like post-birth, project completion calls for:

- Celebration and acknowledgment (bonding with creation)

- Integration of lessons learned (recovery)

- Rest before next creative cycle (restoration)

- Gratitude for the process (spiritual connection)

Birth Wisdom for Daily Life

Pain vs. Suffering: Birth taught me that intensity isn't suffering when it serves a purpose. The same principle applies to all challenging work—difficulty isn't misalignment if it's moving you toward something meaningful.

Surrender vs. Passivity: Birth requires active surrender—fully engaging while letting the larger process lead. This balance of effort and trust applies to every area of aligned living.

Natural Timing: Birth happens when the baby is ready, not according to external schedules. Similarly, your pivotal breakthroughs often emerge from internal timing rather than forced deadlines.

Body Wisdom: During birth, I trusted my body completely—no overthinking, no second-guessing physical instincts. This taught me that the body holds intelligence that the mind cannot access.

Future Applications and Evolutionary Potential

Next-Generation Frequency Technology

Brain-Computer Interface Integration:

- Direct neural feedback for real-time frequency adjustment

- Thought pattern recognition aligned with astrological transits

- Brainwave entrainment customized to individual chart patterns

Quantum Field Measurement:

- Biofield photography showing energetic states

- Quantum interface measurement in real time

- Environmental frequency optimization based on personal needs

Genetic Frequency Mapping:

- DNA analysis reveals optimal frequency ranges

- Epigenetic expression influenced by planetary transits

- Personalized nutrition and supplementation based on astrological constitution

Collective Frequency Applications
Community Frequency Networks:

- Neighborhood energy grids supporting collective well-being

- City planning incorporating astrological and geographical frequencies

- Global meditation networks synchronized with planetary events

Educational System Integration:

- Learning schedules adapted to individual energy cycles

- Curriculum prototyped around natural developmental frequencies

- Classroom environments optimized for frequency coherence

Healthcare Evolution:

- Medical treatments timed to astrological and biological cycles

- Frequency prescription for specific health conditions

- Prevention protocols based on predictive frequency analysis

Planetary Frequency Harmony

Environmental Restoration:

- Ecosystem healing using planetary frequency resonance

- Agricultural cycles optimized for cosmic timing

- Climate change mitigation through frequency intervention

Species Communication:

- Animal communication using frequency translation

- Plant growth optimization through frequency agriculture

- Ocean and forest restoration using sound healing

Consciousness Evolution Through Frequency

The ultimate potential of Frequency Intelligence extends beyond personal optimization to collective consciousness evolution:

Global Coherence: When enough individuals live in alignment with their Frequency Blueprints, we create coherence fields that support planetary healing and evolution.

Intergenerational Healing: Frequency work allows us to heal ancestral trauma and plant seeds of wisdom for future generations through conscious energy transmission.

Species Integration: As we become more frequency-aware, we can communicate and collaborate more effectively with other forms of consciousness—plants, animals, and even planetary intelligence.

This isn't science fiction. It's the natural evolution of consciousness when we stop overriding our energetic nature and start living in harmony with the cosmic frequencies that surround and interpenetrate our existence.

Your Frequency Blueprint is not just a personal tool—it's your contribution to a more coherent, aligned, and conscious world. Every time you honor your natural rhythm instead of forcing productivity, you add to the collective field of humans living in harmony with natural law.

Every time you make a decision from inner alignment rather than external pressure, you strengthen the morphic field of authentic leadership. Every time you rest when your body asks for rest, you give others permission to honor their own cycles.

This is how individual frequency work becomes planetary healing. This is how personal alignment becomes collective evolution. This is why your blueprint matters—not just for your success, but for the conscious evolution of our species.

Final Integration—Living as Frequency

As we complete this comprehensive exploration of your Frequency Blueprint, remember that this isn't just information to understand— it's a living system to embody.

Your blueprint is not a prescription to follow rigidly, but a conversation partner to dance with. Some days you'll feel perfectly aligned with your cosmic timing. Other days, you'll need to find creative ways to honor your energy within life's demands.

The goal isn't perfection—it's precision. The goal isn't control—it's conscious collaboration with the forces that are already moving through your life.

You were born with a frequency. You've been broadcasting it your entire life. Now you have the tools to tune in clearly, amplify what serves you, and share your unique energetic gift with the world.

The age of hustle is ending. The age of frequency has begun. You are part of the leading edge of this consciousness shift, using ancient wisdom and modern technology to create a life that honors both your humanity and your divinity.

Your blueprint is waiting. Your frequency is calling. Your time is now.

The Long Road of Saturn

When I look back, I can see a thread running through my life—one I didn't recognize at the time. It wasn't random. It was timing. Saturn's timing.

I didn't know then that Saturn is called the planet of structure and discipline, the cosmic taskmaster that tests our foundations. Even so, I felt it. Saturn doesn't punish. It reveals. It shows you where you're building on sand, where you're out of sync, and where you've chosen from logic rather than alignment. It does this not once, but in long cycles that eventually push you back to your truth.

For me, that lesson began in my twenties.

At the time, every decision I made was based on what looked right on paper. What school taught. What society validated. I followed the script perfectly: I bought the house, developed the career, and created the picture of success. From the outside, it looked flawless. On the inside, it was hollow.

That's the first signal of dissonance: when achievement doesn't land in your body.

Later, I thought I had corrected course. I left that life behind, created ReyRey, my sustainable fashion brand, and poured myself into building something with beauty and meaning. It felt closer to alignment, but Saturn was still at work. Because even there, I realized I was yet again playing by external ideals, just with a more sophisticated mask.

Saturn teaches us this: misalignment isn't always failure. Sometimes it looks like success, but without sovereign pacing. Saturn forces you to feel the gap. To confront the discomfort of doing all the "right" things while continuing to feel off.

That, in the end, is what eventually brought me to Frequency Intelligence.

Frequency Intelligence is the practical framework I catalyzed from these lessons. It takes what Saturn shows in decades and compresses it into a system you can use now:

Resonance and dissonance as early warning signals	Blueprint analysis to see where you're aligned— and where you're not	Timing literacy so you don't spend years forcing what isn't yours

Not all success is alignment. Not all meaning is embodiment. Saturn was my teacher, but Frequency Intelligence is the method.

What's more, if you're reading this, wondering why something still feels "off" even if everything looks fine, you're not behind. You may just be on Saturn's schedule. The difference now is that with Frequency Intelligence, you don't have to wait twenty years to see it. You can read the signals in real time.

In the next chapter, we'll explore how to translate this blueprint into daily practice through advanced flow states, energy body integration, and the more transcendent mysteries of frequency living that take this work from understanding into embodied mastery.

CHAPTER 5

The Four Frequency Dimensions

The Emotional Body Your Vibrational Compass

The Inner Architecture of Alignment

In 2023, a strange season unfolded—radically reshaping my understanding of human energy systems.

Everything in my life looked fine—my family, my business, my health. Though surprisingly, inside, I was angry, irritated, tired, and unsettled. It was as if something was buzzing under my skin, and I couldn't find the off switch. I searched everywhere for a cause—stress, conflict, overwork—but nothing made logical sense. In truth, my body wouldn't lie. My energy was off, and I knew it.

I went to my mentor, friends, and even clairvoyants. I asked, searched, begged for clarity. Nothing worked—until I stopped trying to fix it and started feeling it. I was experiencing one of the worst periods of my life emotionally, and only later would I understand why: I wasn't in the wrong place—I was in a Reflect cycle. My emotional body was shedding something old that my mind couldn't yet identify.

That was when I truly understood something that would become foundational to Frequency Intelligence: We are not just one body. We are four interconnected frequency dimensions.

Most systems focus on just one dimension—mindset coaching addresses thoughts, fitness targets the physical, therapy explores emotions, or spiritual practices connect you to something greater. However, the Frequency Intelligence approach recognizes that catalytic transformation occurs when all Four Frequency Dimensions are in alignment, speaking the same language, and moving in the same direction.

Your emotions are not problems to be managed, fixed, or overcome. They are messages from your energetic system, rising and falling like waves that carry information about your alignment, boundaries, needs, and truth. When your emotional body is in flow, you feel connected, expressive, present, and emotionally available. When it's blocked or consistently overridden, you feel numb, reactive, overwhelmed, or emotionally suppressed.

Many people, especially those trained in analytical or strategic thinking, are scared of their emotions because they seem irrational, unpredictable, or inconvenient. Keep in mind, emotions aren't interruptions to your logical process. They are information from your vibrational intelligence, often arriving before your mind can construct explanations for what your system already knows.

When I was younger, I often dismissed my emotional responses in favor of strategic decision-making. I was raised to be analytical, studied business, and was trained to make choices based solely on logic and data. Subsequently, time after time, those data-backed decisions failed me: I lost money, time, and energy because I had ignored the intelligence that lived in my gut, my heart, my emotional body's immediate responses to situations and people.

The more I ignored emotional intelligence in favor of purely rational analysis, the more I suffered. I would say yes to opportunities that looked perfect on paper but felt wrong in my system, enter partnerships that made strategic sense but drained my energy, and pursue goals that my mind endorsed but my heart couldn't sustain.

Nothing worked—until I stopped trying to fix the emotional storm and started feeling it fully. I discovered that the message my emotional body was sending wasn't that I was broken or failing. Instead, I was in a natural Reflect cycle, and my emotional system was releasing something old that no longer served my evolution. The itch in my stomach, the inexplicable irritation, the emotional eating patterns—none of it was pathology. It was frequency friction, the natural turbulence that occurs when your system is upgrading itself.

Your emotional body doesn't need logic or justification. It needs permission to be felt, expressed, and honored as a source of intelligence rather than an obstacle to overcome. The emotions that seem to arrive "for no reason"—sudden anger, unexplained sadness, waves of irritation—are often your system's way of processing energetic shifts that your conscious mind hasn't yet recognized.

Signals of emotional misalignment include mood swings that feel disconnected from circumstances, emotional numbness or the inability to access feelings, overreacting to minor situations, difficulty connecting authentically with others, and the tendency to suppress or explain away emotional responses rather than listening to their guidance.

Frequency Intelligence supports your emotional body through daily emotional pattern tracking, offering insights based on planetary transits and numerological cycles that help contextualize emotional waves. It provides specific frequency audio interventions—such as 396 Hz for emotional release or 528 Hz for heart coherence—that nurture your emotional system and support smoother integration.

Remarkably, the most powerful tool for emotional body alignment is permission: permission to feel what's present without immediately trying to change it, permission to express emotions through movement, sound, or creative expression, and permission to trust that emotional responses often carry information that logic hasn't yet accessed.

You are not just a physical vessel carrying around thoughts and emotions. You are a complex, energetic system composed of four distinct yet interconnected frequency dimensions: the Physical Dimension (your biological foundation), the Emotional Dimension (your vibrational compass), the Mental Dimension (your pattern decoder), and the Spiritual Dimension (your source connection). These dimensions influence how you feel, how you act, how you recover, and how you create. They hold your vitality, your triggers, your intuition—and your power.

Your frequency is not just a spiritual concept floating in abstract space. It is a living expression of your entire inner system, and that system communicates through symptoms, sensations, feelings, and intuitive knowings. When these frequency dimensions are ignored or overridden, they begin to whisper, then speak, then scream. This chapter is about decoding those signals so you can live, lead, and love in total alignment with who you actually are beneath all the noise.

Why Most People Live in Energetic Misalignment

We're taught to check our calendars, not our cycles. To track our steps, not our frequency. To plan with logic alone, ignoring the wisdom that lives in our bodies, our emotions, and our innate knowing. We're conditioned to think our way into decisions rather than feeling our way back to truth.

The result is an epidemic of high-functioning misalignment—people who look successful from the outside while feeling hollow, restless, or energetically depleted on the inside. We've been trained to override our natural rhythms in the service of systems that treat humans like productivity machines rather than complex, energetic beings with their own internal timing and intelligence.

Be that as it may, you can't think your way into energetic truth. You have to feel your way back. The Four Frequency Dimensions give us the map for that return journey.

The Physical Body Your Frequency Foundation

This is the body most people live in—until it breaks down. Your physical body is your biological frequency, the vessel that houses your nervous system, hormones, sleep cycles, digestive patterns, and movement rhythms. It's the most tangible and measurable layer of your energetic system, and often the first to signal when something more nuanced falls out of alignment.

When your physical body is in balance, you feel strong, grounded, clear, and energetically sustainable. When it's not, you feel tired, foggy, wired but exhausted, or physically inflamed—symptoms that are often the downstream effects of energetic misalignment rather than purely biological issues.

For me, the first time I understood this connection viscerally was in February 2018, after I had experienced two abortions within a month of each other. My body felt overheated, overused, done. Though I was mentally and physically exhausted, I could not sleep. Something was broken inside me, at a level rest couldn't reach.

That's when I began going to bed every night with hypnosis meditations—a practice I maintained for three months. Slowly, I started to recover. The meditations didn't "fix" me in some mechanical sense; they returned me to myself. They brought me back into rhythm. I began to sleep again. My nervous system softened. My mind began to rest. This taught me something fundamental: your body stores the history of your soul—every trauma, every skipped rest cycle, every override of its natural intelligence.

Your physical body is not a productivity machine to be optimized and driven beyond its limits. It's your frequency translator, constantly converting energetic information into physical sensations and symptoms. When you push through misalignment, your body keeps the score through sleepless nights, tight chest sensations, unexplained headaches, skin breakouts, chronic tension, or that particular kind of fatigue that rest can't seem to touch.

The physical body speaks in signals: pain without injury, exhaustion that rest can't fix, restlessness that movement can't settle, cravings and emotional eating patterns, and trouble sleeping despite being tired. When these symptoms arise, your body is often telling you that something in your energetic system needs attention—not more caffeine, not more productivity, not more pushing through.

Frequency Intelligence integrates your physical body through real-time biofeedback tracking—Heart Rate Variability, sleep quality, stress indicators, and movement patterns. It then offers personalized interventions such as breathwork protocols, light frequency therapy, and optimal physical routines tailored to your astrological and numerological cycles.

Even without technology, you can begin to listen. Gentle movement instead of forced exercise. Frequency music—such as binaural beats—helps regulate your nervous system. Conscious breathwork resets your autonomic system. Proper hydration with minerals supports physical balance. Grounding practices reconnect you to natural rhythms.

Your physical body often knows before your mind does. Learning to listen to its subtle communications is the foundation of all energetic intelligence.

The Mental Body Your Pattern Decoder

This is the realm of your thoughts, beliefs, focus, decision-making patterns, and internal narrative. It's your "thinking frequency"—the way your consciousness processes information, creates meaning, and interprets experience. When this body is aligned, you feel mentally clear, sharp, creative, and intentional. When it's out of sync, you spiral into overthinking, lose your sense of possibility, or get trapped in limiting belief systems that no longer serve your growth.

As someone trained in analytical thinking, I lived primarily in my mental body for years, trusting logic above all other forms of intelligence. I learned through repeated experience that the mind without intuition becomes a closed loop—brilliant at analysis but blind to the buried patterns that only the body and emotions can detect.

I came to understand this lesson particularly hard in business when I began making decisions based purely on intuitive knowing in late 2023. I started ending contracts and letting employees go purely because I felt something was energetically off—even when the financial numbers looked strong and the logical case for continuing was clear. I had no "data" to justify these decisions to anyone else, including myself at times. Though deep inside my system, I knew.

This created enormous internal tension because my mental body demanded explanations, proof, and rational frameworks for decisions arising from a different kind of intelligence entirely. The mind may calculate probabilities and analyze outcomes, but only the body knows the truth in real time.

Your mental body is your internal storyteller, constantly interpreting everything through the lens of belief systems, past experiences, conditioning, and memories. When it's running outdated programming—beliefs like "slowing down equals laziness," "saying no is selfish," or "working hard makes you worthy"—it creates mental noise that drowns out your more expansive intelligence.

For years, these beliefs shaped my decision-making process until my mental body became overloaded from trying to force alignment through willpower alone. I started procrastinating on projects I usually loved, resisting opportunities that once excited me, thinking in anxious loops about problems that didn't have logical solutions.

The mental body becomes scrambled when you're energetically misaligned because it confuses force with flow, effort with effectiveness. It makes you feel guilty for resting when your system needs integration, and anxious about slowing down when your natural rhythm calls for reflection.

Signals of mental body misalignment include chronic overthinking and analysis paralysis, negative thought spirals that seem to have their own momentum, resistance to starting projects or making decisions, mental fog that affects your usual sharpness, and shame or guilt around honoring your natural rhythms rather than external expectations.

Interestingly, the mental body can be retrained. This happens through conscious awareness of thought patterns, hypnosis meditations that reprogram limiting beliefs, and vision journaling that connects your thoughts to your underlying purpose. It also involves tracking which thoughts create emotional spikes or physical tension, and clearing outdated belief systems through techniques like frequency tapping or neuro-linguistic programming.

Frequency Intelligence supports your mental body by reframing cognitive patterns based on your current energy state. It offers astrology-based affirmations and mantras that align with your natural cycles, and tracking mental rhythm fluctuations through numerological and biorhythm analysis. This helps you understand when your mind is naturally sharp versus when it needs rest.

The mental body doesn't need to be silenced or controlled—it needs to be recoded with beliefs and thought patterns that support your energetic truth rather than override it.

The Spiritual Body *Your Source Connection*

This is the most subtle energy body, the least measurable by conventional standards, and often the most powerful in terms of guiding you toward authentic alignment. It's your access point to purpose, meaning, intuitive wisdom, and what many call your soul's voice—the layered intelligence that transcends logical analysis and emotional reactivity.

Most people only consciously access their spiritual body when everything else fails, when conventional solutions no longer work, or during moments of crisis that compel them to seek guidance beyond their usual resources. Now, what if you could build your entire life around this electric connection rather than treating it as a last resort?

Since I was a teenager, I've sought answers beyond the visible world. At thirteen, I was already studying astrology with serious intent. At fifteen, I had my first clairvoyant session—ostensibly asking about love, but really seeking a language for the more elusive questions that conventional education couldn't address. Throughout my twenties and thirties, I explored meditation, energy healing, tarot, numerology, and various consciousness practices that helped me navigate the gap between who I was becoming and who the world expected me to be.

For years, I kept this part of myself hidden, believing it wasn't compatible with business leadership, strategic thinking, or the "real world" of entrepreneurship and consulting. Ironically, the more I tried to separate my spiritual intelligence from my practical decisions, the more misaligned I became.

Now, I let my spiritual body lead—not because I've become less strategic, but because I've discovered that this more intricate intelligence contains information that logical analysis alone cannot access. My most aligned decisions—turning down investments that looked perfect on paper, ending business relationships that were profitable but energetically draining, or launching projects like Frequency Intelligence that had no clear market precedent—all came from this body.

The spiritual body communicates through subtle signals that require stillness and attention to detect. These include the sense that "something is missing" even when circumstances look good, feelings of disconnection from your purpose or calling, doubt in your inner voice or intuitive responses, spiritual fatigue that affects your sense of meaning and direction, and resistance to practices that once nourished your soul.

When your spiritual body is nourished and aligned, you experience a particular kind of clarity that transcends circumstantial happiness. It brings a sense of being connected to something larger than yourself. You begin to trust in timing, even when you can't see the wider view. You also gain access to creative solutions that emerge from beyond logical thinking.

Frequency Intelligence supports your spiritual body through guided meditations and rituals that align with lunar and planetary cycles, personalized cosmic downloads and vision activations based on your astrological blueprint, and connection to your life path and archetypal patterns that help you understand your soul's larger purpose within the human experience.

The spiritual body doesn't require elaborate practices or esoteric knowledge to be accessed. It needs space—meditation without agenda, walks in silence, moments of asking your soul what you need to remember today. Pay attention to synchronicities and repeated signs that appear in your environment, and trust in the physical sensations of expansion or contraction that accompany different choices and directions.

This is the most subtle energy body and often the most powerful because it's the difference between knowing your calendar and knowing your calling. The spiritual body doesn't need proof or external validation—it needs space to communicate the guidance that's always available when you create the conditions to receive it.

How the Four Frequency Dimensions Work Together

These frequency dimensions are not separate systems operating independently of one another. They are layered aspects of a unified energetic field that constantly communicates, adjusts, and seeks a beacon. When you're truly aligned, your physical dimension feels light and energetically sustainable. Your emotions flow naturally without getting stuck or overwhelming your system. Your mind is clear, creative, and focused on what matters. Your soul feels connected to a purpose larger than personal survival or success.

When you're misaligned, the opposite occurs: you feel tired, blocked, emotionally reactive, and spiritually lost. You can't "fix" this multidimensional misalignment with just a planner, a workout routine, or positive thinking alone. You need a frequency reset that addresses the entire system.

When one frequency dimension is out of sync, it inevitably pulls the others down because they're all part of the same energetic ecosystem. Think of a day when you didn't sleep well (physical dimension compromised), which led to snapping at someone you care about (emotional dimension dysregulated), which created mental fog and poor decision-making (mental dimension scrambled), which left you feeling disconnected from any sense of meaning or purpose (spiritual dimension offline). That's a cascading full-system misalignment that can't be resolved by addressing only one dimension.

Yet when all four dimensions are attuned and communicating clearly, you feel magnetic rather than drained, clear rather than confused, and powerful in a way that feels sustainable rather than forced. You move with ease because you're no longer fighting against your own system. You feel supported from within because all aspects of yourself are working in harmony rather than pulling in different directions.

Advanced Frequency Dimension Interconnection Patterns

Understanding the complex ways your Four Frequency Dimensions interact enables you to identify misalignment patterns before they escalate into full-system dysfunction— and respond with targeted interventions that address the root causes rather than surface symptoms.

Physical-Emotional Cascade Patterns

When your physical dimension is depleted due to poor sleep, inadequate nutrition, or nervous system dysregulation, your emotional dimension becomes hyperreactive, less resilient to everyday stressors, and prone to emotional responses that feel disproportionate to circumstances. This isn't emotional instability— it's your emotional dimension trying to process stress through a compromised physical foundation.

Conversely, when your emotional dimension is suppressed or overwhelmed—through unexpressed grief, chronic anger, or emotional numbness—your physical dimension manifests symptoms like digestive issues, immune system suppression, chronic tension, or unexplained fatigue. Your body becomes the storage system for emotions that haven't been processed or expressed.

I experienced this cascade dramatically during my 2018 recovery period after the pregnancy losses. My physical dimension was depleted and traumatized, which made my emotional dimension volatile and unpredictable. Minor frustrations would create massive emotional responses because my physical foundation couldn't provide the stability my emotional processing required. The hypnosis meditations were effective because they addressed both dimensions simultaneously—calming my nervous system while providing emotional integration.

Mental-Spiritual Disconnection Patterns

When your mental dimension is overactive—caught in analysis paralysis, worry loops, or excessive planning—it often drowns out the subtle communications from your spiritual dimension. Your mind becomes so loud that you can't hear the quiet guidance that emerges from stillness and receptivity.

This creates a particularly frustrating pattern where you know something is off, but you can't think your way to clarity. You analyze situations from every angle without reaching a resolution because the information you need is coming from your spiritual dimension, which operates beyond logical analysis.

During my 2023 transition period, my mental dimension was working overtime trying to figure out what was wrong with my business, my motivation, my direction. The more I analyzed, the more confused I became because my spiritual dimension was signaling that I needed to trust an entirely different trajectory—one that my logical mind couldn't yet validate or understand.

The breakthrough came when I learned to quiet my mental dimension enough to receive spiritual guidance, then use my mental dimension to translate that guidance into practical steps rather than trying to think my way to insight.

Emotional-Mental Feedback Loops

Your emotional and mental dimensions can create either supportive or destructive feedback loops, depending on whether you're aware of their interaction patterns. When your emotional dimension is dysregulated—through suppressed feelings, emotional reactivity, or numbness—your mental dimension attempts to create logical explanations for emotional states, often generating stories, blame patterns, or limiting beliefs that fail to address the underlying emotional needs.

This creates mental narratives, such as "I'm not good enough" when your emotional dimension actually needs validation or "I can't trust anyone" when you're processing betrayal or disappointment that hasn't been fully felt and integrated.

Conversely, when your mental dimension operates from limiting beliefs or negative thought patterns, it triggers emotional responses of shame, fear, or hopelessness that then reinforce the limiting beliefs, creating a closed loop that's difficult to interrupt through mental effort alone.

The solution addresses both dimensions simultaneously—feeling the emotions fully while consciously choosing thoughts and beliefs that support your healing and growth rather than perpetuate old patterns.

Spiritual-Physical Integration Challenges

Your spiritual dimension provides guidance and direction that often requires physical action and embodiment to manifest in reality. When there's a disconnection between spiritual guidance and physical follow-through—receiving clear intuitive direction but not trusting it enough to act—you experience spiritual frustration and physical stagnation.

This is common for highly intuitive people who receive clear guidance but struggle to trust it enough to make practical changes in their daily lives, relationships, or careers. The spiritual dimension provides the vision, but the physical dimension must carry it out through concrete actions, lifestyle changes, and adjustments to boundaries.

During my decision to decline the 2025 funding, my spiritual dimension was absolutely unwavering, as I knew this wasn't my path. Simultaneously, my physical dimension felt the concern and uncertainty of choosing an unknown direction over a guaranteed opportunity. The integration happened when I learned to trust the spiritual guidance enough to let my physical actions align with it, even when I couldn't see the complete picture.

Multidimensional Healing Approaches

When you understand these interconnection patterns, you can address misalignment more efficiently by working with the dimensions that have the most influence on your particular pattern rather than trying to fix everything at once.

- For physical–emotional cascades: Focus on nervous system regulation through breathwork, gentle movement, and emotional expression practices that help both dimensions return to baseline stability.

- For mental–spiritual disconnection: Practice quieting mental activity through meditation, journaling, or repetitive physical tasks that allow spiritual guidance to emerge. Then use your mental dimension to translate insights into actionable steps.

- For emotional–mental feedback loops: Interrupt the cycle by feeling emotions fully without immediately creating stories about them, then consciously choosing thoughts that support your healing rather than perpetuate victim narratives or limiting beliefs.

- For spiritual–physical integration challenges: Start with small physical actions that honor spiritual guidance—even when you can't see the complete path—building trust between these dimensions through consistent follow-through on intuitive promptings.

This is what Frequency Intelligence makes possible—not perfect balance, which is a static concept that doesn't match the dynamic nature of living systems, but energetic sovereignty, which is the ability to read, interpret, and respond to your own system with precision and trust.

Gender and Cultural Conditioning
How Society Shapes Your Frequency Expression

The way you experience and express your Four Frequency Dimensions has been undeniably influenced by gender expectations, cultural conditioning, and societal programming that often directly conflict with your natural energetic patterns. Understanding these influences is essential for reclaiming authentic frequency expression rather than performing versions of yourself that drain your system while appearing socially acceptable.

Gender-Specific Frequency Suppression Patterns
Women are often trained from early childhood to suppress their physical dimension's natural signals—to smile when they're angry, to accommodate others' needs above their own comfort, to override fatigue in service of caretaking responsibilities. This creates a pattern where women become disconnected from their body's intelligence about boundaries, rest, and authentic desires.

The emotional dimension faces even more complex suppression for women, who are simultaneously told they're "too emotional" while being expected to manage everyone else's emotional needs. This double bind creates internal confusion about whether emotional responses are valid guidance or a sign of feminine weakness, leading many women to suppress their emotional intelligence precisely when they need it most for decision-making and boundary-setting.

Men face different but equally damaging conditioning around frequency expression. The physical dimension is often the only socially acceptable channel for processing stress, leading to over-reliance on physical solutions for emotional or spiritual imbalances. Men are trained to push through physical discomfort, ignore pain signals, and measure worth through physical performance rather than listening to their body's intelligence about rest, vulnerability, or gentleness.

The emotional dimension faces severe suppression for most men, who learn early that emotional expression beyond anger is weakness or instability. This forces emotional processing into the mental dimension, creating intellectual approaches to feelings that bypass the wisdom emotions contain about relationships, authenticity, and personal truth.

Cultural Programming and Frequency Distortion

Different cultural backgrounds create specific patterns of frequency dimension emphasis or suppression that affect how individuals naturally express their energetic intelligence. Cultures that prioritize collective harmony may unconsciously suppress the expression of individual spiritual dimensions in favor of group conformity. In contrast, cultures that emphasize individual achievement may override natural rest cycles and integration needs in the physical and emotional dimensions.

Religious conditioning often creates complex relationships with spiritual dimension expression, sometimes enhancing connection to transcendent intelligence while simultaneously creating shame or fear around personal spiritual authority and direct spiritual experience that doesn't conform to institutional frameworks.

Professional environments frequently demand mental dimension dominance while suppressing emotional intelligence, intuitive decision-making, and spiritual considerations that don't translate into measurable metrics or conventional business logic.

Deconditioning work involves recognizing where societal programming clashes with your natural frequency expression. It means consciously developing practices that honor your authentic energetic patterns, rather than performing socially acceptable versions that drain your system.

For women, this often means reclaiming the right to say no, prioritizing their own physical and emotional needs, trusting their intuitive responses even when others question them, and expressing emotions as a sign of intelligence rather than instability.

For men, frequency reclamation involves developing emotional literacy and expression, learning to interpret physical sensations as guidance rather than obstacles to overcome, and accessing wisdom from the spiritual dimension that transcends achievement-oriented identity.

For all individuals, this process requires examining inherited beliefs about productivity, success, relationships, and self-worth to identify where external programming conflicts with internal truth and authentic energetic expression.

Trauma-Informed Approaches to Frequency Dimension Healing

Stored trauma creates specific disruption patterns in each frequency dimension that require gentle, informed approaches rather than forceful healing methods that may overwhelm an already compromised system. Understanding how trauma manifests across your four dimensions allows you to work with your nervous system's protective patterns rather than against them.

Trauma Manifestations in the Physical Dimension

Trauma often lives in the body as chronic tension patterns, immune system suppression, digestive dysfunction, sleep disturbances, and hypervigilance or numbness that affects your ability to feel safe in your physical form. Your nervous system may be stuck in fight-

or-flight activation or freeze responses that made sense during traumatic experiences. Now they interfere with your ability to relax, digest, sleep, or feel pleasure in your body.

Physical dimension trauma healing requires approaches that work with your nervous system's timing rather than forcing it to release patterns before it feels safe to do so. This includes gentle movement practices that help you reconnect with your body without overwhelming sensation, breathwork that supports nervous system regulation without triggering hyperventilation or panic responses, and touch-based healing modalities that respect boundaries and consent.

Progressive muscle relaxation, gentle yoga, swimming, or walking in nature can help your physical dimension remember safety and pleasure without demanding immediate transformation or emotional processing that your system may not be ready to handle.

Emotional Dimension Trauma Patterns

Trauma frequently creates emotional dysregulation patterns. These include:

Emotional numbness: where you lose access to your feeling responses.	Emotional flooding: where normal situations trigger overwhelming emotional reactions.
Emotional reactivity: where your responses feel disproportionate to current circumstances.	Emotional confusion: where you can't distinguish between past trauma responses and present-moment feelings.

Emotional dimension healing requires creating safety for feeling without being overwhelmed by emotions, learning to distinguish between trauma responses and current emotional guidance, developing tools for emotional regulation that don't suppress authentic feelings, and gradually expanding your capacity to process difficult emotions without being flooded or shut down.

This might include working with a trauma-informed therapist who understands nervous system regulation, practicing emotional release through creative expression or movement, and learning to provide yourself with the comfort and validation your emotional dimension needs to process stored experiences safely.

Mental Dimension Trauma Responses

Trauma often creates mental patterns, including hypervigilance, where your mind constantly scans for danger or problems, negative thought loops that replay traumatic experiences or create worst-case scenarios, limiting beliefs about safety, trust, and self-worth that were adaptive during trauma but now restrict your choices and possibilities, and dissociation where your mental dimension disconnects from emotional or physical experience to avoid overwhelming sensation.

Mental dimension trauma healing involves gently challenging limiting beliefs while respecting the protective function they originally served, developing present-moment awareness that helps distinguish between trauma responses and current reality, and creating new neural pathways through practices like therapy, meditation, or somatic experiencing that help your mind feel safe to relax its hypervigilant patterns.

Spiritual Dimension Trauma Impact

Trauma can create spiritual disconnection, including loss of trust in divine timing or universal intelligence, feeling abandoned by a higher power or spiritual guidance, difficulty accessing the sense of meaning or purpose that transcends personal survival, and spiritual bypassing, where spiritual practices are used to avoid feeling or processing trauma rather than integrating it.

Spiritual dimension healing often requires reconnecting with practices, beliefs, or communities that feel genuinely nourishing rather than obligatory, developing trust in timing and unfolding that doesn't require you to have everything figured out, and finding meaning-making frameworks that honor your trauma experience as part of your spiritual journey rather than evidence of spiritual failure.

Integrated Trauma-Informed Frequency Work
The most effective trauma healing addresses all Four Frequency Dimensions simultaneously while respecting your nervous system's capacity and timing. This means working with your physical dimension to create safety and regulation, honoring your emotional dimension's need to process at its own pace, gently retraining your mental dimension to distinguish between past and present, and reconnecting with your spiritual dimension as a source of resilience and meaning.

Frequency Intelligence approaches trauma-informed healing by tracking patterns across all four dimensions, offering interventions that support nervous system regulation rather than overwhelming already compromised systems, and providing gentle guidance that respects your healing timeline rather than pushing for immediate transformation.

Seasonal and Life Phase Frequency Variations

Your Four Frequency Dimensions don't operate in static patterns. They shift and evolve through natural cycles that include monthly lunar phases, seasonal changes, astrological transits, and monumental life transitions that require different energetic approaches and support systems.

Monthly Lunar Cycle Impact on Frequency Dimensions
The lunar cycle creates a predictable pattern of energetic emphasis that affects how your four dimensions naturally want to express and what kinds of activities feel most aligned during different moon phases.

During the New Moon phase, your spiritual dimension is naturally more receptive to vision, intention-setting, and new beginning energy, while your mental dimension benefits from planning and goal clarification. Your physical dimension may feel lower energy but more intuitive, and your emotional dimension often feels clean and clear, making this an ideal time for starting new projects or setting intentions that align with your deeper purpose.

The Waxing Moon phase activates your physical and mental dimensions for action, implementation, and building momentum around projects or goals initiated during the New Moon. Your emotional dimension feels optimistic and expansive, while your spiritual dimension provides ongoing guidance and course-correction as you move toward your goals.

Full Moon energy amplifies all four dimensions, often intensifying whatever patterns are already present—heightened creativity and manifestation if you're aligned, or emotional overwhelm and physical agitation if you're out of sync. This phase is optimal for completion, celebration, and releasing what no longer serves your evolution.

The Waning Moon phase emphasizes your emotional and spiritual dimensions for processing, integration, and releasing old patterns or relationships that have completed their purpose in your life. Your physical dimension may naturally want more rest, and your mental dimension benefits from reflection rather than active planning.

Seasonal Frequency Shifts

Your frequency dimensions respond to seasonal changes in light, temperature, and natural rhythms that affect hormone production, nervous system regulation, and emotional patterns, whether you're conscious of these influences or not.

Spring energy naturally activates your physical and mental dimensions for new projects, increased social connection, and creative expression. Your emotional dimension feels hopeful and expansive, while your spiritual dimension provides vision and inspiration for what you want to create during the coming year.

Summer amplifies your physical dimension's capacity for activity, social engagement, and visibility while supporting your emotional dimension's expression through joy, playfulness, and connection. This season favors outward action and brings to life the projects initiated during spring's planning phase.

Fall emphasizes your mental and emotional dimensions for evaluation, completion, and preparation. This season supports reflection on what you've created during the active months, the release of projects or relationships that no longer serve your evolution, and gentle preparation for winter's introspective energy.

Winter naturally draws energy into your spiritual dimension, inviting reflection, inner work, and a more attuned connection to meaning and purpose. Your physical dimension needs more rest and gentleness, your emotional dimension processes stored experiences from the year, and your mental dimension benefits from contemplation rather than active problem-solving.

Life Phase Transitions and Frequency Evolution

Major life transitions create temporary or permanent shifts in how your frequency dimensions express and what they need for optimal function and integration.

Pregnancy and early motherhood dramatically affect all four dimensions: The physical dimension undergoes regenerative changes that demand a comprehensive lifestyle adjustment. The emotional dimension processes identity shifts and protection instincts. The mental dimension often feels scattered or different from pre-pregnancy cognitive patterns. The spiritual dimension may feel either deeply connected to the energy of creation or temporarily inaccessible due to physical demands.

Career transitions, whether voluntary or involuntary, typically activate your mental and spiritual dimensions as you process identity changes and seek new purpose or direction, while creating temporary instability in your physical and emotional dimensions as you navigate uncertainty and change.

Relationship changes—whether through marriage, divorce, or loss—stir your emotional and spiritual dimensions as you revisit attachment patterns and the meaning you assign to love and connection. These shifts often ripple through your physical dimension as stress responses and reshape your mental dimension through changes in daily routines, focus, and future orientation.

Health challenges or aging invite an integrative connection to the spiritual dimension, even as they call for shifts in expectations and care within the physical dimension. These transitions often catalyze revolutionary shifts in priorities and values that affect all aspects of frequency expression.

Understanding that your frequency dimensions naturally evolve and require different support during life transitions prevents the frustration of trying to maintain static practices or energy patterns during periods when your system is naturally reorganizing itself in response to new circumstances and growth.

Business and Leadership Applications
Leading from Frequency Intelligence

The Four Frequency Dimensions framework transforms how you approach leadership, team dynamics, organizational culture, and business decision-making by recognizing that sustainable success requires energetic alignment at both individual and collective levels.

Individual Leadership Through Frequency Dimension Awareness Traditional leadership training focuses on external skills—such as communication techniques, strategic planning, and performance management—while overlooking the energetic foundation that determines whether those skills feel authentic and sustainable or forced and depleting. Leading from frequency dimension awareness means making decisions based on your whole system rather than just mental analysis, which consistently produces better outcomes with less personal strain.

When your physical dimension is aligned, you naturally command presence and authority—without performing confidence or projecting energy you don't genuinely possess. People feel your groundedness and stability because it emanates from your nervous system, not from your personality or effort.

Your emotional dimension in alignment creates authentic charisma and connection because you're not suppressing feelings or performing emotional states that don't match your internal experience. Team members feel safe being authentic around you because you model emotional intelligence and honest communication rather than professional facades.

Mental dimension alignment produces clear thinking, creative problem-solving, and decision-making that integrates logical analysis with intuitive intelligence. Your strategic thinking feels inspired rather than effortful because you're accessing broader intelligence than pure rational processing.

Spiritual dimension connection infuses your leadership with purpose and meaning that transcends personal ego or short-term results. You make decisions based on a long-term vision and authentic values rather than reacting to market pressure or competitive dynamics.

Team Dynamics and Collective Frequency Management

Understanding frequency dimensions allows you to recognize that team dysfunction often results from energetic misalignment rather than skill deficits or personality conflicts. When team members are operating from different frequency dimensions without aware-ness, miscommunication and conflict become inevitable.

Some team members may be naturally physical dimension-dominant, preferring hands-on work, clear action steps, and tangible results over abstract planning or emotional processing. Others operate primarily from their mental dimension, excelling at analysis, strategy, and complex problem-solving but potentially overlooking emotional intelligence or intuitive factors.

Emotionally dominant team members often provide valuable insights into team dynamics, client relationships, and the human impact of business decisions. Spiritual dimension-focused individuals may contribute vision, purpose, and innovation that transcends conventional industry thinking.

Effective team leadership involves recognizing each person's natural frequency dimension strengths while ensuring that essential decisions integrate wisdom from all four dimensions rather than over-relying on one approach.

Organizational Culture and Frequency Integration

Most organizational cultures unconsciously suppress certain frequency dimensions while overemphasizing others, creating a systemic misalignment that manifests as burnout, high turnover, poor decision-making, and a lack of innovation or authentic purpose.

Companies that operate primarily from mental dimension values—analysis, efficiency, logical problem-solving—often suppress emotional intelligence and spiritual consideration, leading to cultures that feel soulless or unsustainable despite strong financial performance.

Organizations that prioritize metrics tied to the physical dimension—productivity, output, measurable results—may over-look the emotional and spiritual needs of employees, creating environments where people feel like task performers rather than whole human beings.

Integrating frequency dimension awareness into organizational culture involves creating policies and practices that honor natural human rhythms, encouraging emotional intelligence alongside analytical thinking, supporting spiritual purpose and meaning alongside profit goals, and designing work environments that support all four dimensions rather than demanding constant activation and performance.

Business decisions made from only one frequency dimension—typically mental dimension analysis—often miss crucial information that other dimensions provide about timing, people, values, and long-term sustainability.

Physical dimension input includes information about energy sustainability, resource requirements, and whether a decision can be realistically implemented given current capacity and circumstances.

Emotional dimension intelligence provides insight about relationships, team dynamics, customer experience, and whether decisions align with authentic values rather than just strategic objectives.

Mental dimension analysis contributes logical evaluation, risk assessment, strategic planning, and systematic thinking about implementation and outcomes.

Spiritual dimension wisdom offers a perspective on purpose, meaning, timing, and whether decisions serve evolution and growth or merely maintain the status quo comfort and security.

Integrating all four dimensions into decision-making leads to more holistic choices—ones that honor practical needs, emotional intelligence, logical analysis, and spiritual alignment—resulting in decisions that feel intelligent and sustainable, rather than merely smart but depleting.

Case Study: Transforming a Misaligned Team

I consulted with a technology company whose leadership team was experiencing chronic conflict despite strong individual performance and clear strategic objectives. Traditional team coaching had focused on communication skills and role clarification without addressing the underlying energetic dynamics that were creating friction.

When I introduced frequency dimension assessment, the pattern became clear: the CEO was operating primarily from his mental dimension, making decisions through analytical frameworks that ignored emotional intelligence and team members' spiritual needs for meaning and purpose. The creative director was an emotional dimension-dominant individual, providing valuable insights into user experience and team morale, but often felt unheard when emotional considerations were dismissed as "soft" or irrelevant to business objectives.

The technical lead operated from his physical dimension, excelling at implementation and practical problem-solving but becoming frustrated when asked to engage in strategic planning or visionary thinking that didn't connect to concrete action steps. The marketing manager was spiritual and emotionally dimension-focused, contributing innovative ideas and brand vision, but struggling with the data-driven culture that didn't value intuitive market intelligence.

Rather than trying to change anyone's natural frequency dimension strengths, we created decision-making processes that intentionally gathered input from all four dimensions before making important choices. Within three months, team conflict decreased dramatically while innovation and employee satisfaction increased because everyone's energetic intelligence was being recognized and utilized rather than suppressed or ignored.

This case illustrates how frequency dimension awareness transforms group dynamics by honoring different types of intelligence rather than forcing everyone to operate from the same energetic approach.

Energy Leaks vs. Energy Flow *Understanding Systemic Patterns*

When one of your frequency dimensions is misaligned, it creates energy leaks that drain your entire system, pulling the others down through interconnected pathways that operate below conscious awareness. Understanding these leak patterns enables you to identify where your energy is hemorrhaging and take targeted action to restore systemic flow.

Think of a day when you didn't sleep well, which compromised your physical dimension's ability to regulate stress and emotion. This led to snapping at someone you care about because your emotional dimension couldn't process ordinary frustration through a depleted physical foundation. The emotional reactivity then created mental confusion and self-criticism, which disconnected you from any sense of spiritual purpose or meaning. That's a full-system energy leak cascading through all four dimensions.

Conversely, when your frequency dimensions are aligned and communicating clearly, you experience systemic energy flow—a state where you feel magnetic rather than effortful, clear rather than confused, and powerful in a way that feels sustainable rather than forced. You move with ease because you're no longer fighting against your own internal intelligence. You feel supported from within because all aspects of yourself are working in harmony rather than competing for resources or attention.

This is what Frequency Intelligence makes possible—not perfect balance, which is a static concept that doesn't match the dynamic nature of living systems, but energetic sovereignty, which is the ability to read, interpret, and respond to your own system with precision and trust.

Advanced System Learning How Frequency Intelligence Evolves with You

Your Frequency Intelligence system isn't static—it evolves with you as it learns your unique patterns, responses, and what actually works for your specific energetic design rather than applying generic recommendations that may not match your individual needs.

The more you engage with daily check-ins and track your responses to different practices, timing recommendations, and energetic guidance, the more the system learns your particular frequency signature and refines its recommendations accordingly.

Suppose the system notices that you're consistently drained during high-energy Mars transits that typically support action and leadership. It begins by suggesting rest and inner work during those periods, rather than encouraging visibility or bold action that misaligns with your energetic pattern. Let's say your mood tracking reveals that you journal most effectively during Waning Moon phases rather than New Moon intention-setting periods. The system then creates custom prompts and reminders during your optimal emotional processing windows.

When your Heart Rate Variability consistently spikes after listening to specific frequency tones or practicing certain breathwork techniques, those interventions become integrated into your personalized daily reset recommendations.

You're no longer guessing how to care for yourself or trying to force your unique system into generic wellness templates. You're collaborating with technology that learns your energetic language and responds with recommendations that feel personally relevant and practically effective.

This creates a feedback loop of increasing energetic intimacy and trust in your own system as you see concrete evidence of what supports your frequency and what depletes it, building confidence in your internal guidance while providing external validation and structure for trusting your energetic intelligence.

The Vision A World That Lives by Frequency Intelligence

What would happen if everyone developed fluency in their Four Frequency Dimensions? If energetic literacy became as fundamental as reading and writing? If we systematized our families, schools, workplaces, and communities around human frequency rather than mechanical productivity?

We would stop forcing ourselves and each other through arbitrary timelines that ignore natural rhythms and individual energetic design. We would stop performing productivity and start practicing presence, awareness, and responsive alignment with what our systems actually need for sustainable high performance and genuine fulfillment.

Instead of raising children to override their natural patterns in service of external expectations, we would teach them to ask questions like "Am I in my Launch zone today?" instead of "What's on my schedule?" We would normalize conversations about energetic states and timing as practical intelligence rather than mystical concepts.

Professional environments would support statements like "I'm in a reflection cycle—let's wait until next week to make this decision," or "My nervous system needs integration time before I can give you clear feedback on this proposal," or "The planetary energy is supporting deep work today—let's postpone the brainstorming session until our creative window opens."

This represents a fundamental shift from treating humans like productivity machines that should perform consistently regardless of internal state, to recognizing that optimal performance emerges from alignment with natural rhythms, energetic readiness, and timing that honors both individual patterns and collective dynamics.

This isn't fantasy or utopian thinking—it's the logical evolution of human consciousness as we develop a more sophisticated understanding of how energy, timing, and awareness affect everything from individual well-being to organizational effectiveness to global harmony.

Embodied Frequency *Living Your Truth Daily*

The fundamental transformation happens not in the big moments of insight or major life decisions, but in the daily micro-choices that either honor or override your energetic intelligence. It's in the way you speak to yourself when you make a mistake, how you respond to unexpected challenges, whether you push through fatigue or honor your need for rest, and your willingness to trust internal guidance even when it conflicts with external pressure or expectations.

As you develop frequency dimension literacy, you begin to notice patterns in your own system that were previously invisible: You make better decisions in the morning when your mental dimension is clear, rather than forcing choices during your natural afternoon emotional processing time. Certain relationships consistently drain your emotional dimension, while others restore it. Your creative projects flow when they align with your spiritual dimension's sense of purpose rather than just mental planning. Your physical dimension has its own intelligence regarding timing, boundaries, and which activities support versus deplete your system.

This awareness transforms everyday moments into opportunities for alignment. The morning rituals that feel authentic to your rhythm rather than imposed by external templates. The midday pause to check in with your system instead of pushing through energy dips. The evening practices that help your nervous system transition from activation to rest rather than carrying the day's tension into your sleep.

Your story becomes one of energetic embodiment: "The morning rituals most people do, I do at night. That's when I finally feel the house go quiet. That's when I journal, light candles, talk to myself, and call in my clarity. I've learned to trust my intuition more than the numbers. Even though I was taught to lead with data in school, business, and strategy, some of my worst decisions came from ignoring the feeling in my gut. Now, I check in with myself constantly. Like the Princess and the Pea—I feel the pebble in my stomach, and I ask it what it needs."

This is not about perfecting a daily schedule or optimizing your performance through better habits. It's about building intimacy with your frequency—learning to read your own signals with the same attention you might give to understanding a complex business problem or nurturing a meaningful relationship.

Integration and Evolutionary Potential

The Four Frequency Dimensions framework represents more than a personal development tool. It's a foundation for conscious evolution that has implications for how we structure society, education, healthcare, business, and human relationships around energetic truth rather than mechanical efficiency.

As individuals develop frequency dimension literacy, they naturally create ripple effects in their families, teams, and communities by modeling what it looks like to honor natural rhythms, trust internal guidance, and make decisions from a place of wholeness rather than fragmentation or reactive patterns.

The ultimate goal isn't individual optimization but collective coherence—communities of people who understand their own energetic patterns and can collaborate from a place of mutual respect for different frequency expressions, timing needs, and ways of contributing to shared goals and vision.

When you develop mastery of your own Four Frequency Dimensions, you don't just improve your personal life—you become part of a larger shift toward honoring human energy as sacred intelligence that deserves respect, attention, and responsive care rather than constant override in service of external demands or artificial timelines.

Your frequency dimension awareness becomes a contribution to collective consciousness that supports everyone's return to energetic sovereignty, authentic expression, and alignment with the natural rhythms that govern sustainable growth, creativity, and well-being.

In the next chapter, we'll explore how to apply these foundational principles to your professional life, creative work, and leadership style—translating personal energetic alignment into sustainable success that honors your frequency while creating meaningful impact in the world around you.

The Physical Dimension
Your Energetic Foundation

Your physical dimension is your frequency vessel—the biological foundation that translates energetic information into physical sensations, symptoms, and signals. It houses your nervous system, which processes everything from emotional stress to environmental input, your hormonal cycles that affect energy, mood, and mental clarity, and your circadian rhythms that govern when you're naturally alert, creative, or ready for rest.

This body operates according to measurable patterns and cycles that can be tracked, analyzed, and optimized when you understand how to listen to its communications. Unlike the other energy bodies, the physical body offers concrete feedback that can be quantified—Heart Rate Variability, sleep quality, cortisol levels, and inflammation—all of which reflect your energetic alignment.

The physical body often signals misalignment before your conscious mind recognizes what's happening. You might notice chronic fatigue that doesn't improve with rest, indicating that you're energetically depleted rather than just physically tired. Restlessness or overstimulation that makes it challenging to settle suggests your nervous system is dysregulated. Sleep disturbances, digestive issues, or hormonal imbalances that conventional medicine can't fully explain. Unexplained aches, tension patterns, or inflammatory responses that seem disconnected from physical causes.

When I was going through the emotional turbulence of 2023, my physical body was the first to signal that something more complex needed attention. I felt tired even after sleeping, unmotivated even when there was meaningful work to do, and I found myself eating more—not from physical hunger but as a way to soothe an unnamed discomfort that lived somewhere between my stomach and my heart.

I learned to respond to these signals not with more discipline or effort, but with practices that supported my nervous system's return to integration: gentle movement that honored my energy level rather than forcing intensity, frequency music and binaural beats that helped regulate my autonomic nervous system, conscious breathwork that reminded my body how to rest, proper hydration with mineral support for my adrenals, and grounding practices that reconnected me to natural rhythms rather than artificial timelines.

Frequency Intelligence tracks your physical body through wearable technology that monitors Heart Rate Variability, sleep patterns, stress indicators, and movement quality, while offering personalized interventions based on your real-time data combined with your astrological and numerological patterns. It detects physical energy peaks and dips throughout your natural cycles, recommends custom rituals for nervous system regulation, and teaches you to interpret your body's signals as guidance rather than problems to be solved.

Your physical body often knows before your mind does, and learning to honor its intelligence rather than override it is the foundation of sustainable high performance and creative fulfillment.

The Emotional Dimension
Your Vibrational Compass

Your emotions are the language of your energetic system— not random biochemical events to be managed or controlled, but sophisticated messengers carrying information about your alignment, boundaries, needs, and more introspective truths that your logical mind hasn't yet processed. They rise and fall like tides, sometimes gently lapping at the shores of your consciousness, sometimes arriving like storms that demand your complete attention.

146

When your emotional body is in flow, you feel connected to yourself and others, emotionally expressive without being reactive, and present with whatever feelings arise without being overwhelmed by them. When it's blocked, suppressed, or chronically overstimulated, you feel numb to your own experience, reactive to circumstances that wouldn't usually affect you, overwhelmed by feelings that seem too big for the situation, or emotionally suppressed to the point where you can't access your own responses.

This is particularly challenging for people who've been trained to prioritize rational analysis over emotional intelligence, especially women who've been called "too emotional" when they were actually being too intuitive for linear systems that ignore the subtle information that emotions provide about timing, relationships, and alignment.

For years, I tried to separate my emotional responses from my business decisions, believing that professional effectiveness required emotional detachment. But this created a split in my system that ultimately undermined both my personal well-being and my professional intuition. The decisions that looked most logical often felt energetically depleting, while the choices that my emotional body endorsed—even when they seemed risky or unconventional—consistently led to better outcomes.

During that confusing emotional spiral in April 2023, I was experiencing classic signs of emotional body misalignment:

Mood swings that felt disconnected from external circumstances	Emotional numbness alternating with overwhelming sensitivity
Overreacting to minor situations while feeling nothing about major life events	Difficulty connecting authentically with people I usually felt close to

Instead of trying to think my way out of the emotional turbulence, I began tracking patterns: which planetary transits corresponded with my emotional waves, how my feelings shifted throughout my monthly cycle, which environments or conversations left me feeling drained versus energized. I realized that what felt like emotional chaos was actually my system processing a significant life transition that my conscious mind wasn't ready to acknowledge.

The emotional body holds truth before the mind can explain it. It contracts around people, situations, or choices that aren't aligned with your highest path, even when those people or situations look perfect from a logical standpoint. It expands around opportunities, relationships, or directions that support your authentic expression, even when the practical details aren't yet evident.

Frequency Intelligence supports your emotional body through daily emotional pattern tracking that correlates your feelings with planetary cycles, numerological influences, and personal biorhythms, offering contextual insights that help you understand emotional waves as information rather than pathology, and providing specific frequency audio interventions like 396 Hz for emotional release, 417 Hz for facilitating change, or 528 Hz for heart coherence.

Practical emotional body alignment includes allowing yourself to feel without immediately trying to fix or change emotional states, expressing emotions through movement, sound, journaling, or creative outlets, conducting regular "gut check" meditations where you place your hands on your stomach and ask what information your emotional body is holding, and trusting that emotional responses often contain guidance about people, situations, or timing that your logical mind hasn't yet processed.

Your emotional body doesn't need management—it needs listening. When you honor its intelligence, it becomes one of your most reliable guidance systems for navigating complex decisions and relationships.

The Mental Dimension *Your Pattern Decoder*

Your mental dimension encompasses your thoughts, beliefs, decision-making frameworks, focus patterns, and the internal narrative that shapes how you interpret experience and create meaning from the constant stream of information flowing through your consciousness. This is your "thinking frequency"—not just intellectual capacity, but the quality, clarity, and alignment of your mental processes.

When your mental body is aligned, you experience mental clarity that cuts through complexity, creative problem-solving that generates solutions from beyond conventional thinking, intentional focus that naturally prioritizes what matters most, and decision-making that feels both logical and intuitively correct. When it's out of sync, you get caught in mental spirals that drain energy without producing insight, lose your sense of possibility or creative vision, experience analysis paralysis that prevents action, or operate from limiting beliefs that constrain your choices.

The mental body is particularly susceptible to conditioning from educational systems, cultural programming, and family patterns that may not align with your natural way of processing information and making decisions. For those of us trained in analytical environments, there's often an over-reliance on mental processes at the expense of other forms of intelligence, creating a kind of cognitive exhaustion that no amount of mental effort can resolve.

During my transition period in 2023, I experienced classic mental body misalignment: My usually sharp thinking became foggy and uncertain. I found myself procrastinating on decisions that would have been straightforward in the past. I got caught in negative thought loops about my business and personal direction. Additionally, I felt resistance to projects and opportunities that my mind knew were valuable, but my system couldn't energetically sustain.

The breakthrough came when I realized that my mental body wasn't malfunctioning—it was trying to process a fundamental shift in direction that required integration beyond pure logical analysis. The mental confusion wasn't a problem to be solved through more thinking; it was a signal that my system was recalibrating around new priorities and possibilities that didn't yet fit my existing mental frameworks.

Your mental body becomes scrambled when you're energetically misaligned because it's trying to create logical explanations for experiences that originate from emotional, physical, or spiritual intelligence. It confuses force with flow, interprets energetic resistance as personal failure, and fosters guilt or anxiety around natural rhythms that are not in sync with external expectations or timelines.

Mental body misalignment shows up as chronic overthinking that doesn't lead to clarity, negative thought spirals that seem to have their own momentum, resistance to starting projects or making decisions that used to feel straightforward, mental fog that affects your usual cognitive sharpness, and shame or guilt around honoring your natural energy patterns rather than pushing through with willpower.

The mental body can be realigned through practices that integrate thinking with feeling: hypnosis meditations that reprogram limiting beliefs at the subconscious level, conscious dialogue with yourself that's loving rather than critical, vision journaling that connects your thoughts to your more revealing purpose and values, tracking which thoughts create emotional spikes or physical tension, and clearing outdated belief systems through techniques that address both cognitive and energetic patterns.

Frequency Intelligence supports your mental body by reframing cognitive patterns based on your current energy state—rather than forcing thought processes that don't match your natural rhythm. It offers astrology-based affirmations and mantras aligned with your personal cycles and planetary influences, and tracks headspace clarity through numerological and biorhythm analysis, which helps you discern when your mind is naturally sharp versus when it benefits from rest or a shift in mind-centered activity.

The mental body doesn't need to be silenced or controlled through force—it needs to be recoded with beliefs, thought patterns, and decision-making frameworks that support your energetic truth rather than override it with outdated programming.

The Spiritual Dimension Your Source Connection

This is the most subtle frequency dimension, the aspect that connects you to purpose, meaning, intuitive guidance, and what many traditions call your soul's voice—the intelligence that transcends personal identity while informing your most authentic choices and creative expression. It's your access point to the wisdom that flows through you rather than from your personal effort or analysis.

The spiritual body operates beyond the measurable metrics that govern the physical, emotional, and mental dimensions. Yet its influence on your life direction, creative inspiration, and sense of meaning is often the most profound. This is the body that whispers "this isn't it" about opportunities that look perfect from every external angle, that guides you toward people, places, and projects that align with your more unalterable purpose, and that provides the kind of knowing that doesn't require external validation or logical proof.

Most people unconsciously access this intelligence during pivotal life moments, such as career transitions, relationship changes, creative breakthroughs, or periods of loss that force them to question fundamental assumptions about life direction and meaning. But the spiritual body is always available as a guidance system when you understand how to create the conditions for receiving its communications.

Since I was young, I felt a natural connection to what others might call the invisible or mystical dimensions of existence. Throughout every major transition in my life—from ending my long-term relationship to walking away from investment opportunities that didn't feel aligned—this more kinetic intelligence provided guidance that my logical mind couldn't access and my emotional body could only sense as expansion or contraction around different choices.

My most aligned decisions, including the development of Frequency Intelligence itself, emerged not from strategic planning but from this deeper source of knowing—the kind of guidance that arrives as a download, a vision, or a sudden clarity about direction that feels both surprising and inevitable.

The spiritual body communicates through signals that require presence and stillness to detect:

A sense that something essential is missing, even when external circumstances appear successful	Feelings of disconnection from your destined purpose or calling	Resistance to silence, solitude, or practices that once connected you to something greater than personal concerns
Doubt in your inner voice or loss of trust in intuitive responses	Spiritual fatigue that affects your relationship to meaning and wonder	

When your spiritual body is aligned and nourished, you experience what many describe as flow states—not the psychological concept of optimal performance, but the existential experience of being connected to creative intelligence that flows through you rather than from your personal effort. You feel guided rather than driven, inspired rather than effortful, and connected to timing that unfolds with a precision that logical planning alone cannot achieve.

Frequency Intelligence supports your spiritual body through guided meditations and ritual practices that align with your personal astrological cycles and lunar phases. It also offers personalized cosmic downloads and vision activations based on your birth chart and numerological patterns. These tools illuminate your connection to your soul's archetypal journey and life path themes—providing context for your personal experiences within larger cycles of growth and service.

The spiritual body doesn't require elaborate practices, special knowledge, or mystical experiences to be accessed—it needs space and permission. Simple practices include meditation without an agenda or specific outcomes, walking in silence while remaining open to insights or guidance, asking your soul questions before sleep, and paying attention to dreams or morning insights. Notice synchronicities or repeated symbols that appear in your environment. Begin trusting the physical sensations of expansion around choices that align with your determined purpose versus contraction around opportunities that look good but don't feel right.

This is the energy body that distinguishes between knowing your schedule and knowing your calling, between managing your life and being guided by your life's more charged intelligence.

Real-World Case Study *Paul's Transformation*

Paul isn't spiritual by nature—he's analytical, observant, methodical in his thinking. For years, he felt stuck in his career trajectory, neither unhappy with his work nor inspired by it. He sensed that something was missing, but was unable to articulate what needed to change or how to access the clarity he was seeking.

He had tried conventional approaches: career coaching that focused on skills and market opportunities, productivity systems that promised better time management and goal achievement, and strategic planning exercises that mapped his professional development in relation to industry standards and logical progression.

None of these approaches addressed what was actually happening: his four energy bodies were sending different signals that he didn't have the language to interpret. His physical body felt restless during work hours, but he couldn't identify what kind of movement or environment would feel better. His emotional body felt flat about opportunities that looked promising on paper. His mental body was sharp and capable, but uninspired by the problems he was solving. His spiritual body felt disconnected from any sense of deeper purpose or calling in his professional life.

When I ran his complete Frequency Blueprint—integrating his astrological patterns, numerological cycles, and energetic tendencies—something clicked immediately. The assessment didn't offer him a new career path or strategic plan; it gave him language for patterns he had been feeling but couldn't name. It showed him that his restlessness wasn't a sign of professional dissatisfaction but a reflection of energetic misalignment; his need for variety and intellectual stimulation was part of his natural rhythm rather than professional instability; and his intuitive responses to workplace dynamics were valuable intelligence—not emotional reactivity.

Within hours of reading his blueprint, I saw the shift in his energy. He had softened, relaxed, and settled into himself in a way I hadn't seen in months. He didn't say much about the specific insights, but I could feel that something had moved inside him—a recognition, a permission, a remembering of patterns he had always known but never trusted.

This is the power of addressing all four energy bodies simultaneously rather than trying to solve energetic misalignment through mental analysis alone. Paul didn't need more career strategy; he needed energetic literacy—the ability to read his own signals and trust them as guidance rather than problems to be overcome.

Practical Tools for Daily Frequency Dimension Awareness

The goal of frequency dimension awareness isn't to achieve perfect balance across all four aspects—that's a static concept that doesn't match the dynamic nature of living systems. Instead, the practice is developing energetic literacy: the ability to read what each dimension is communicating, understand how they influence each other, and respond with practices that support your system's natural intelligence rather than override it.

Daily Frequency Dimension Check-In Practice:
Each morning, before checking your phone or engaging with external demands, take three minutes to scan your Four Frequency Dimensions:

Physical: How does my body feel today? What does it need: movement, rest, nourishment, or stillness?

Emotional: What emotions are present right now, and what might they be telling me about my current situation or decisions I need to make?

Mental: What's the dominant thought pattern in my mind, and is it supporting my clarity or creating noise?

Spiritual: Do I feel connected to something larger than my immediate concerns, or do I feel isolated and purposeless?

Evening Integration:
Before sleep, reflect on how each frequency dimension shifted throughout the day: What dimension felt most aligned today, and what supported that alignment? What dimension felt most off, and what circumstances or choices contributed to that misalignment? What did I learn about my natural rhythms and needs? How can I better support my system tomorrow?

The Inner Compass Practice:
Create a dedicated space in your journal or use the Frequency Intelligence app when available for more in-depth tracking. Each morning, rate your alignment from 1–10 in each frequency dimension, then ask what would bring each dimension into greater transmission today. You don't need perfect tens across all aspects—

you only need awareness of where you are and permission to respond accordingly.

For the Physical Dimension: gentle movement that matches your energy level, breathwork for nervous system regulation, frequency music or binaural beats, hydration with mineral support, and grounding practices in nature

For the Emotional Dimension: journaling without editing or censoring, emotional release through sound or movement, gut check meditations, permission to feel without immediately trying to change emotional states, and creative expression that honors what's present

For the Mental Dimension: hypnosis meditations for belief reprogramming, loving self-dialogue rather than critical internal commentary, vision journaling that connects thoughts to a more gravitational purpose, tracking thought patterns that create emotional or physical responses, and clearing limiting beliefs through energetic techniques

For the Spiritual Dimension: meditation without agenda or goals, walking in silence while remaining open to guidance, asking questions before sleep, paying attention to morning insights, noticing synchronicities and environmental signs, and trusting expansion and contraction around different choices.

When You Ignore the Energy Bodies

When you consistently override your energy bodies in service of external expectations, productivity demands, or cultural conditioning that treats humans like machines, life becomes increasingly effortful and unsustainable. You experience miscommunication because you're not communicating clearly with yourself, anxiety because you're fighting against your natural rhythms, burnout because you're depleting your system faster than you're restoring it, regret because decisions made without energetic awareness often don't align with your authentic priorities, and a general sense of being out of sync with your own life.

Most people aren't broken, mentally ill, or lacking in capability. They're simply living from the outside in, making choices based on external templates rather than internal guidance, scheduling their lives according to artificial timelines rather than natural rhythms, and measuring success according to metrics that may not align with their energetic truth.

This book and the Frequency Intelligence system exist to reverse that pattern: giving you back your compass and reminding you that your energy is not random but readable, not chaotic but cyclical, not a problem to be managed but intelligence to be trusted.

What Living in Your Frequency Actually Looks Like

What does it actually look like to live in your frequency—day by day, moment by moment?

It doesn't look like a strict ritual, a color-coded planner, or a mandatory 5 a.m. wake-up call that ignores your natural circadian rhythms. It doesn't look like the perfectly crafted morning routines you see on social media or the rigid productivity systems that treat every human the same, regardless of their unique energetic design.

It looks like flow. Joy. Clarity. Presence. It looks like me, in alignment—music on, candles lit, laughing in the kitchen while cooking something special, work flowing easily without force or resistance, ideas coming fast and clear, and playing more with my children because I want to, not because I should or because some parenting philosophy told me it was optimal.

On those days, I feel like the world is my oyster. There's a lightness in my body that doesn't depend on external circumstances. My energy is warm and happy from the inside out. My thoughts are generous rather than critical. There's no inner resistance, no feeling of pushing against invisible barriers—only movement that feels natural and sustainable.

That's what a regulated frequency feels like—not a constant high-vibration state that requires effort to maintain, but a natural ease that emerges when your choices align with your energetic truth.

I've learned that when I'm in alignment, everything softens without losing its power. There's ease without laziness, strength without force, productivity without burnout. I don't feel like I have to hustle or prove anything to anyone. I move authentically—and everything meets me there because I'm operating from synergy rather than compensation.

This state isn't achieved through perfect discipline or flawless execution of ideal practices. It emerges from developing energetic intimacy with yourself—learning to read your own signals, trust your own timing, and honor your own rhythm even when it doesn't match external expectations or conventional timelines.

My Personal Daily Frequency Tools

Over years of experimentation and refinement, I've developed a collection of practices that consistently help me return to alignment when I feel off-center and maintain cohesiveness when I'm already in flow. These aren't rigid requirements but flexible tools that I use intuitively based on what my energy bodies are communicating on any given day.

Journaling has become my primary method of emotional and mental body integration. I write from love rather than obligation, using ink and paper to manifest clarity and process whatever emotions or thoughts need expression. These aren't structured entries with prompts or goals—they're honest, raw, real check-ins with whatever is present in my system without trying to fix or change it immediately.

Hypnosis meditation, particularly at night, provides deep nervous system rewiring that my conscious mind can't access during waking hours. These meditations work with my subconscious patterns while my mental body is relaxed, allowing for integration of new beliefs and emotional patterns that support my frequency rather than override it.

Frequency music and binaural beats shift my energy without requiring words, analysis, or mental effort. Different frequencies serve different purposes—some for focus and mental clarity, others for emotional release or spiritual connection. They work directly on my nervous system and energy field, bypassing the mental body's tendency to analyze or resist change.

Crystals, incense, and essential oils create environmental frequencies that support my system's natural intelligence. I surround myself with scents, stones, and subtle energies that feel safe and nourishing to my spiritual body, understanding that our environment constantly influences our internal state, whether we're conscious of it or not.

Astrological check-ins help me understand my current energetic weather by looking at planetary transits affecting my natal chart. I track my timing through cosmic cycles, letting celestial patterns guide my decisions about when to initiate, when to rest, when to push forward, and when to surrender control and trust the unfolding.

Mentorship and guidance remain vital, though increasingly I'm becoming my own voice of clarity as my energetic literacy develops. I still speak with mentors I've trusted for years, but more and more, I'm learning to trust the guidance that lives within my own system instead of constantly seeking external validation or direction.

When I feel disconnected from my frequency, it usually begins in the mental body, characterized by overthinking, doubt, or analysis paralysis. I used to think misalignment was always physical—just too much work or not enough rest—but I've learned that it's more often mental overload or emotional dissonance. The moment I go against my intuition, override my gut response, or agree to something out of expectation rather than authentic truth, I feel the energetic glitch immediately. It pulls me off frequency in ways that no amount of self-care can fix until I address the core misalignment.

When that happens, I come back to center through stillness and listening. I sit quietly and ask my system what needs attention, what needs to be released, or what decision needs to be reconsidered. Over time, I've developed what I call an inner screen—like a visionary interface behind my eyes that provides immediate guidance when I close them and ask a direct question. The answer flashes up in bold yellow light: *YES. NO. MAYBE. WAIT.*

This might sound mystical, but it's actually the natural intelligence that emerges when you begin to trust yourself again, rather than constantly seeking external validation for internal knowing. As my confidence in this process grew, my inner guidance system became more sophisticated and detailed. Now it shows me scenarios, energetic previews, and subtle clues about timing and direction that help me navigate complex decisions with precision and confidence.

This is what I call Energetic Intelligence, or FQ—the ability to read your own system accurately and respond with choices that support your natural frequency rather than override it.

Designing Your Day with Energetic Precision

Transformation is not a lightning strike that happens once and changes everything forever—it's a rhythm that develops through consistent micro-alignments, daily attunement to your energetic state, and the willingness to make small course corrections that honor what your system is communicating rather than what external demands are requiring.

It lives in your breath, your awareness, your willingness to pause and check in with yourself before reacting to circumstances or other people's urgency. The way you begin and end your day determines everything in between because these transitional moments set the energetic tone for how you'll navigate challenges, opportunities, and decisions throughout your waking hours.

In this expanded exploration, we move beyond insight and into embodiment—where your Frequency Blueprint becomes a lived practice rather than just an interesting concept. This isn't about adding more tasks to your already packed schedule; it's about learning to tune in to your energetic state and make micro-shifts that align you with your own rhythm every single day.

The Myth of the Perfect Morning

Let's drop the fantasy that social media has created around morning routines and spiritual practices: you don't need a ninety-minute sunrise ritual with matcha preparation, cold plunges, breathwork sequences, journaling prompts, and meditation cushions to access energetic alignment.

You need a moment. Of stillness. Of noticing. Of choosing your energy before the world chooses it for you.

Your "morning ritual" might happen at 10 p.m., once the house is finally quiet and you can return to yourself without interruption. That's not just okay—that's honoring your actual life circumstances rather than forcing yourself into someone else's ideal that doesn't match your reality.

For me, as a mother of three young children, most mornings are about getting everyone fed, dressed, and out the door without major meltdowns—not sipping adaptogenic mushroom tea in contemplative silence while watching the sunrise through floor-to-ceiling windows.

In reality, my real frequency attunement begins when the house goes still, when the children are asleep, the emails are closed, and I get to return to the conversation with myself that runs underneath all the daily logistics and responsibilities.

Transformation doesn't come from one dramatic shift or perfect execution of ideal practices. It comes from the accumulation of small alignments: the way you speak to yourself when you make a mistake, how you respond to unexpected challenges, whether you honor your energy levels or push through them, and your willingness to make choices based on internal guidance rather than external pressure.

This is about turning energetic theory into a daily rhythm, anchoring your Frequency Blueprint into your lived experience through practices that work with your actual life rather than the life you think you should be living.

The Daily Flow System: Practical Energetic Navigation

Frequency Intelligence operates as a living guide that helps you practice your energy awareness rather than understand it through intellect alone. Your personal operating system becomes embodied through consistent attention to your energetic state and willingness to adjust your choices, timing, and responses based on what your four energy bodies are communicating.

Each day within the Frequency Intelligence framework follows a guided structure that adapts to your natural rhythms while providing the consistency your nervous system needs to develop energetic literacy and trust in your own internal guidance.

Morning Alignment: Setting Your Energetic Intention

The goal of morning alignment is tuning into your energetic weather before the world pulls you into reaction mode, obligation, or other people's priorities and timelines.

Your Daily Frequency Score emerges from the integration of cosmic alignments affecting your natal chart, your personal numerological cycle, your biorhythms based on your birth date, and any wearable biofeedback data if you're using integrated technology.

Your Elemental Energy Zone indicates whether your system is naturally oriented toward:

Fire energy:	Earth energy:
action, leadership, visibility	grounding, practical completion, steady progress

Air energy:	Water energy:
communication, mental clarity, social connection	intuition, emotional processing, creative flow

This tells you what mode your system is prepared to work in rather than forcing an energetic approach that creates resistance.

Action Guidance provides specific direction about whether today supports strategy and planning, rest and integration, launching and visibility, or reflection and recalibration, helping you make scheduling decisions that work with your energy rather than against it.

Suggested Rituals are personalized based on your astrological patterns combined with your current emotional and physical state—perhaps solar breathwork when your system needs activation, grounding audio when you're feeling scattered, or heart coherence meditation when you need emotional regulation.

For example: "Today's Frequency Score is 77. The Moon is conjunct your natal Sun, amplifying your natural leadership and creative expression. Your Personal Day 3 indicates that creativity and communication are flowing optimally. This is an ideal day for teaching, sharing your vision, or leading important conversations. Suggested morning ritual: Take a three-minute voice recording to activate your throat chakra and prepare your voice for clear expression."

Midday Micro-Reset: Recalibration During Natural Energy Shifts

The midday recalibration addresses the natural energy fluctuation that occurs in most people's circadian rhythms, typically between 1–3 p.m., when blood sugar, cortisol, and attention naturally dip regardless of how well-aligned your morning was.

The system provides gentle alerts when your Heart Rate Variability drops below your personal baseline, when your emotional tone shifts based on your tracking patterns, or when significant cosmic transits like Mars square Neptune become exact and may affect your energy, mood, or decision-making clarity.

These moments invite micro-practices rather than major interventions: conscious breathing that resets your nervous system, listening to a specific frequency tone based on your personal profile and current needs, or taking one aligned micro-action like setting a boundary, expressing a feeling, or moving your body in a way that feels nourishing rather than forced.

For example: "You're entering an emotional processing phase based on your cycle tracking and current lunar position. Take ninety seconds for yourself. Listen to your personalized 528 Hz heart harmonic tone while repeating the mantra: 'I am safe in stillness, and my sensitivity is my strength.'"

Evening Integration: Reflection and System Recovery

Evening integration focuses on reflection, logging your energy patterns for future reference, and supporting your system's natural recovery processes through practices that help your nervous system shift from activation to rest.

The app prompts you to log your mood, energy levels, and alignment throughout the day, reflect on any patterns of resistance or breakthrough that emerged, track emotional or physical responses to decisions you made, and choose a calming reset practice such as lunar audio frequencies, guided visualization, or simply sitting in silence.

For example: "Your day showed 80 percent alignment with minor resistance during your 2 p.m. meeting. Tomorrow features a waxing moon in your eleventh house, combined with a Personal Day 5. Prepare for expansion in your social connections and collaborative projects. Suggested evening ritual: candlelight meditation with 396 Hz soundbath for releasing any tension from today's interactions."

Now that you understand your inner architecture, we'll explore how to translate this awareness into daily practice. In the next chapter, we'll dive into the practical application of living your Frequency Intelligence—hour by hour, decision by decision, breath by breath.

You'll discover how to start your day in energetic alignment, shift between flow zones when your energy changes, use music, movement, and meditation as tuning tools for different energy body needs, and create daily rituals that work with your natural rhythm rather than against it.

This is where theory becomes embodiment, where understanding becomes living practice. Alignment isn't about perfection—it's about presence, awareness, and the willingness to honor what your system is telling you moment by moment.

When all four energy bodies are attuned and communicating clearly, you don't feel like you're managing your life—you feel like you're living it from the inside out, guided by intelligence that's both ancient and immediate, both personal and connected to something infinitely larger than individual concerns.

You don't need to fix every aspect of yourself. You just need to start listening to the conversation that's already happening within your own energetic system.

CHAPTER 6

The Old Questions
The New Intelligence

We enter life into a script.

Before we ever speak, there are expectations already coded into us: family ideals, cultural traditions, school rankings, and career hierarchies. We learn quickly that some paths are considered "good," others are deemed "risky," and almost all are judged by identical metrics: output, achievement, and visibility.

This is what I call the Old System—not because it's ancient, but because it operates from assumptions that no longer serve the complexity of modern human potential. Through my work helping individuals reclaim their authentic direction and building ReyRey as an international brand, I have discovered how this system represents the accumulated conditioning of industrial thinking, survival programming, and social structures that prioritize collective efficiency over individual alignment.

The Old System doesn't ask you what feels alive. It asks you what looks successful. It doesn't inquire about timing or rhythm. It demands to know if you're moving fast enough. It doesn't care about alignment. It measures whether you appear impressive.

The seismic irony is that most of us live entire decades governed by these questions without realizing we never consciously chose them. They were inherited through family systems, reinforced by educational institutions, and standardized across cultural environments. They form the invisible operating system that runs our organizations, shapes our family dynamics, and drives our personal ambitions.

Yet this unconscious automation creates predictable costs that we've learned to normalize:

Leaders are running teams on manufactured urgency instead of allowing them to operate on their natural rhythm.	Individuals trapped in cycles of burnout are treated as personal inadequacy rather than systemic dysfunction.
Parents unconsciously teach children that achievement matters more than alignment.	Our society has normalized diagnosis, medical leave, and psychological collapse because our foundational systems never accounted for the reality of human frequency.

Frequency Intelligence enters this landscape not as another motivational framework or productivity optimization tool, but as a fundamental replacement for the questions that shape reality. It offers inquiries that measure resonance instead of optics, timing instead of pressure, coherence instead of constant output.

Early Signal *When a Child Feels the Mismatch*

I felt it as early as age 10–12—a quiet sense that I was living some-one else's life. Even then, without language to name it, I recognized there was an invisible script, not written by me, that I was expected to perform. While I couldn't yet call it "the Old System," I knew something didn't feel like mine.

Dancing became my unconscious rebellion. I was extremely active during my younger years, throwing myself into movement, rhythm, and performance. Looking back, I now understand that dance was one of the ways I instinctively stayed connected to my own frequency. It allowed me to feel relational rhythm in my body, to follow rhythm instead of rules, to experience alignment even in a world that was teaching me to override it. Without realizing it, I was training my system to notice timing, to move with cycles, and to trust flow rather than force.

This early awareness was not unique to me. Working with individuals from diverse cultural backgrounds, I have discovered that many report similar childhood experiences—moments when they sensed a fundamental mismatch between what they were being asked to become and what felt authentic to their nature.

The pattern consistently reveals itself: the educational foundation most of us received was designed around administrative convenience rather than human developmental needs. By the time a child enters formal schooling, they have already absorbed assumptions that will govern their relationship to time, energy, achievement, and self-worth for decades. They learn that value derives from standardized performance metrics. They discover that comparing themselves to classroom hierarchies is not only acceptable but expected. They internalize the notion that speed, productivity, and efficiency represent moral virtues while slowness, reflection, and individual rhythm are perceived as problems requiring correction.

What gets systematically excluded from educational foundations isn't just content—it's rhythm:

Learning to recognize and trust natural energy patterns	Developing the capacity to distinguish between external pressure and genuine internal motivation
Making decisions based on timing and alignment rather than fear of falling behind arbitrary schedules.	Understanding when the body, emotions, or cognitive systems require rest and recalibration instead of continued performance

This programming isn't implemented with malicious intent. It represents the sincere efforts of parents, teachers, and institutional leaders who are passing on what they themselves have learned. In any case, the systematic message remains clear: children are not taught to trust their frequency. They are trained to override it in the service of institutional requirements and social expectations.

What I lived personally is not just my story—it is the echo of history. To understand why so many of us lose ourselves in adulthood despite having early clarity, we must examine the systems that shaped us long before we had the language for self-awareness and alignment.

To a large extent, awareness in childhood doesn't guarantee protection. Even when we sense the mismatch early, the pull of the Old System is strong, and many of us eventually get caught in its gravity.

The Lost Decade When Conditioning Wins

Even for someone like me—who resisted early on and felt like a misfit as a child—the Old System still found a way to pull me in.

Around age twenty, as I entered adulthood, I lost sight of my own path. Despite the instincts I had as a teenager, I began to follow the script I had once resisted. I studied what looked good on paper, pursued the goals that fit expectations, and measured myself against the benchmarks society held up as worthy. From the outside, I was correct and reasonable. On the inside, I was drifting away from the rhythm that had once felt so alive in dance.

That decade—my twenties into my early thirties—was marked by achievement that felt strangely hollow. I had willingly chosen all of it, but it was still scripted. The irony is sharp: the very thing I had resisted in childhood became the life I was unconsciously living.

This was also something I identified while working with individuals who felt trapped despite external success. I can recognize this pattern everywhere. Financial success triggered by energy extraction rather than sustainable contribution—essentially converting well-being into money through methods that could not be maintained long-term. The exhaustion isn't physical—it's the soulful fatigue that comes from living out of alignment with your authentic nature.

This pattern of early awareness followed by systematic conditioning reveals how the Old System operates. It doesn't eliminate natural frequency awareness—that would be impossible. Instead, it teaches us to mistrust our internal signals while rewarding conformity to external standards. By the time we reach adulthood, we have often internalized this override as accepted, responsible behavior. The script becomes automatic: push through resistance, perform regardless of internal state, achieve external markers of success, repeat indefinitely.

The cost compounds over time. What begins as childhood adaptation to institutional requirements evolves into adult patterns that systematically disconnect us from the internal guidance systems that would otherwise support sustainable success, authentic relationships, and meaningful contribution. We learn to function efficiently while drifting out of alignment, achieving impressive external results while experiencing internal disconnection and dissatisfaction.

It wasn't until I began breaking the script again in my thirties, and fully reclaiming alignment in my forties, that I could see how deeply the Old System had shaped me. At 41, I now recognize that what I felt at 10–12 was not rebellion—it was clarity. A knowing that my life had to be written from resonance, not from inheritance. This arc—early awareness, temporary loss, conscious reclamation—mirrors what most individuals I work with have experienced. It's not weakness to get pulled in by the Old System. It's proof of how powerful and pervasive it is. What matters is whether you learn to recognize it, reclaim your rhythm, and consciously choose again.

My story was personal, but it wasn't personal at all. It was systemic.

To comprehend why so many of us lose ourselves, we have to zoom out to the structures that trained us long before adulthood.

The Historical Evolution
From Factory Time to Algorithmic Time

Understanding how we arrived at this point requires examining the historical progression that created our current relationship to time, productivity, and human value. I discovered how each phase of this evolution embedded specific conditioning patterns that still operate in people's nervous systems today.

During the Industrial Age, human activity became organized around the requirements of machines rather than human needs. Time was reconceptualized as linear, uniform, and measurable in ways that served manufacturing efficiency but ignored individual biological rhythms, creative cycles, and energy patterns. The definition of "productive workers" became those who could generate identical output at a consistent pace, regardless of their natural fluctuations in focus, creativity, or motivation.

This period established the foundational assumption that human value could be accurately quantified through standardized performance metrics. This assumption continues to govern educational, organizational, and social systems despite mounting evidence of its limitations and costs.

The Managerial Age professionalized these control mechanisms, developing increasingly sophisticated systems for measuring, predicting, and optimizing human output. Efficiency has transformed from a practical consideration into a moral imperative, with a faster pace and increased volume consistently positioned as inherently superior regardless of long-term sustainability, quality considerations, or human well-being costs. Leadership became synonymous with control rather than attunement to collective intelligence and appropriate timing.

The Digital and Algorithmic Age has refined these same principles through technological amplification. We replaced factory bells with notification systems, transformed visibility into professional currency, and converted human attention into the primary raw material for generating economic value.

Each evolutionary phase has reinforced the same core logic: optimize the human being for maximum output. The methods became more sophisticated, but the fundamental premise remained consistent. Human beings should function as predictable, consistent, measurable units of productivity rather than complex adaptive systems that require different approaches depending on natural phases and timing.

Frequency Intelligence challenges this foundational premise. While working with individuals to reclaim their natural timing, I discovered that we are not linear devices optimized for consistent productivity. We are cyclical systems that require different approaches, different energy management strategies, and different success metrics depending on natural phases and developmental timing.

When we attempt to treat cyclical beings as linear machines, we generate predictable system failures: individual burnout, creative stagnation, and what I call "high-functioning dysfunction." This is the ability to maintain impressive external performance while experiencing chronic internal stress, anxiety, and disconnection from authentic purpose and sustainable energy patterns.

These historical patterns don't just live in textbooks—they live in us. They show up in the very questions we ask ourselves each day, the silent scripts running in the background of our choices.

The Questions That Shape Reality
Old System vs. Frequency Intelligence

Every cultural system reveals its deepest assumptions through the questions it teaches people to ask automatically. The Old System has trained us to interrogate ourselves with specific inquiries so consistently that we rarely notice they represent conditioning rather than natural human curiosity.

Yet these questions determine how we evaluate opportunities, measure progress, define success, and make the thousands of micro-decisions that compound into our overall life experience. They operate as invisible software running in the background of decision-making processes, creating predictable patterns of anxiety, competition, and exhaustion that most people accept as inevitable aspects of ambitious living.

Questions from the Old System

The Old System operates through inquiries configured to measure performance against external standards while systematically ignoring internal alignment, natural timing, and sustainable energy management.

How much financial revenue did you generate last year, and does that amount provide sufficient evidence of your professional worth?

This inquiry reduces the entire spectrum of human contribution—creativity, collaboration, problem-solving, emotional intelligence, cultural impact, relationship building—to a single quantitative metric. This leads to strategic decisions based primarily on how numerical outcomes will appear to external observers rather than what actually serves authentic contribution capacity.

What do other people think about your success, and what strategies are you implementing to ensure they recognize your achievements?

This question transforms genuine accomplishment into performance anxiety by positioning external perception as the primary arbiter of value and meaning. Constant image management can be psychologically exhausting, making it harder to focus on the actual work itself.

Are you visible enough, productive enough, and active enough to maintain relevance in your professional field?

This creates the compulsion to accept every opportunity, networking event, and collaboration request out of fear that absence equals irrelevance. The result is chronic exhaustion, superficial work output, and complete disconnection from the creative vision that originally motivated the career.

What strategies are you implementing to scale impact, accelerate growth, and optimize every hour for maximum productivity?

This transforms life into a productivity optimization experiment, creating chronic anxiety about whether current efforts are "enough" while disconnecting from the natural rhythms that actually support sustainable high performance.

Who is achieving more success than you in your field, and what strategies are they implementing that you haven't incorporated?

This turns professional development into competitive stalking, measuring authentic journeys against other people's marketing materials and transforming collaboration into a form of competi-tion. These Old System questions, when analyzed collectively, create urgency, anxiety, and internal fragmentation. They system-atically reward surface-level performance over substantial contri-bution and forced effort over energetically sustainable approaches to achievement. They train us to ignore internal guidance while optimizing for external metrics that may have little relationship to authentic success or meaningful contribution.

Unexpectedly, when I began to ask different questions, everything changed. It wasn't about answering the old ones better—it was about replacing them altogether."

Questions from Frequency Intelligence
The questions of Frequency Intelligence operate from entirely different assumptions about how human consciousness functions, how creativity actually works, and how sustainable success is

created over time. Instead of attempting to override natural patterns, they work in partnership with them.

What quality of energy do I want to experience while creating, and does my current approach align with that intention?

This inquiry prioritizes the subjective experience of your creative process, leading to scheduling creative work during periods when you feel most alive rather than forcing creation during depleted states.

Am I currently in a Launch, Align, or Reflect phase, and what does my current phase require in terms of action and energy allocation?

This honors natural decision-making cycles, helping you avoid evaluating opportunities during reflection periods and resisting hasty decisions during times that call for information gathering.

Does this opportunity match my natural frequency and long-term development trajectory, or is it pulling me off course?

This inquiry cuts through the attractiveness of "good opportunities" to ask more layered questions about alignment, leading to choices that serve both financial reward and personal meaning.

Is my nervous system in a state of relaxed openness, or am I grinding against my natural rhythm?

This treats nervous system state as strategic information rather than something to be ignored, distinguishing between productive intensity and destructive grinding.

Am I building something that naturally expands over time, or am I creating something that requires constant effort to maintain?

This helps distinguish between sustainable momentum and unsustainable force, identifying where natural strengths intersect with genuine market needs.

These FQ inquiries don't chase external outcomes through force and optimization. Instead, they activate internal intelligence, natural timing awareness, and sustainable energy management. They systematically reward depth over speed, sovereignty over approval-seeking, and long-term coherence over short-term impression management.

It's one thing to see these questions on paper, but their impact becomes painfully clear when life gets complicated—when the Old System collides with the unpredictability of reality.

When the System Breaks Down in Real Life

The gap between these two approaches becomes most visible when life gets complex—when the neat frameworks of the Old System meet the messy reality of human experience. I've felt this breakdown ripple through every aspect of my life—business, travel, creation, consumption, even the way entire organizations move around me.

There was a period in 2019 when ReyRey was growing, and I was being pulled in directions that looked like success but felt like chaos—investor meetings, partnership opportunities, speaking engagements, all objectively good developments. Yet I found myself increasingly tired and confused, making decisions from rationale rather than clarity, and losing touch with the creative vision that had originally inspired the brand.

The Old System questions were driving my choices: Are we growing fast enough? How do we stay relevant in a competitive market? How fast can we grow?

These inquiries pushed me toward constant action, external validation, and competitive positioning that left me feeling like a stranger in my own business.

In retrospect, it wasn't just internal pressure creating this dissonance. External forces beyond my control were also revealing the fragility of systems forged on Old System thinking. We had spent several years carefully building relationships with foreign dealers, developing marketing partnerships, and investing significantly in understanding our global consumers' preferences for our handcrafted Italian shoes. The business development had progressed naturally through authentic relationship building and product-market alignment.

Then, overnight, new trade policies and tariff increases eliminated 80–90 percent of our American market revenue. The tariffs made our shoes prohibitively expensive for consumers who had previously been eager customers. Dealer agreements became worthless, planned deliveries were canceled, and marketing investments lost their value—not because of any failure in our business model, product quality, or market demand. These losses stemmed from political leaders making choices based on domestic perception management rather than consideration for the economic ecosystems their policies would disrupt.

This experience revealed a profound disconnect between political timing and business development rhythms. Political systems optimize for electoral cycles and immediate voter response, while authentic business relationships require longer-term development and market cultivation. When these timing systems conflict, the damage cascades through thousands of businesses that have no voice in the policy formation process.

It reinforced my understanding that frequency misalignment operates at every level—from individual decisions to global systems where political timing, economic development cycles, and relationship building operate according to irreconcilably different rhythms.

Moreover, it doesn't stop at business. The same dissonance reveals itself in how we travel, consume, and even search for authenticity in our culture. The Old System has shaped more than our work—it has shaped how we experience life itself.

The Cultural Patterns I've Witnessed

This breakdown between conscious values and unconscious behavior patterns extends far beyond business into every aspect of how we experience and consume culture itself. Through extensive travel over two decades—including extended periods in Kenya, India, Vietnam, Thailand, Mexico, Cambodia, Argentina, Cuba, Uruguay, and Indonesia—I witnessed the transformation from authentic discovery to systematized performance happening in real time.

Travel once represented a path to genuine cultural immersion that required little more than curiosity and an open mind to engage with the unexpected. The spontaneous encounter, the unplanned conversation, the discovery of perspectives that couldn't be researched in advance—these experiences provided education that couldn't be obtained through any other means. Yet just as the Old System had colonized work and education, I watched it reshape even the most intimate experiences of discovery and wonder.

Now people spend weeks planning the "perfect" trip, researching every recommended restaurant and photo location they've seen online. When they arrive, they're so focused on recreating experiences curated by algorithms that they never actually experience the place itself. They come home with great pictures and no real memories. When everyone must experience the same "authentic local culture," authenticity becomes a standardized template rather than a living relationship between visitors and communities.

I've seen this same pattern in how we approach sustainability and conscious consumption. Through ReyRey, business publications emphasized sustainability, ethical production, and transparent supply chains for years. Yet when examining actual consumer behavior, these conversations remained largely theoretical. A potential customer might spend thirty minutes reading about our ethical production methods, then purchase similar shoes from a fast-fashion platform because of price optimization and delivery speed.

This illustrates the Old System's most entrenched programming: despite conscious values and intellectual understanding, unconscious behavior patterns follow convenience and optimization thinking. The analytical mind comprehends sustainability principles, while purchasing decisions remain governed by conditioning that treats price and convenience as the only relevant factors.

What I've discovered is that conscious behavior isn't always activated by education or awareness alone. It often requires disruption that creates emotional activation around identity and values alignment. When external events challenge people's sense of who they want to be associated with, they begin making choices based on resonance rather than pure optimization.

These cultural patterns don't land equally—they shape and scar each generation differently. To understand the scope of the Old System's grip, we have to see how it imprints across time.

The Generational Divide

Different age groups respond to the breakdown of the Old System breakdown in ways that reflect their historical context and developmental conditioning. Each generation carries both wisdom and wounds that shape how they experience this transition.

Boomers and Generation X were conditioned during periods when stability and institutional loyalty represented reliable paths to security. For decades, sustained effort and consistent output were rewarded with predictable advancement. The idea of honoring natural rhythms and timing initially seemed like a luxury—until the realization struck that ignoring these patterns was destroying health and family relationships.

Millennials were promised purpose-driven careers, but they were delivered endless optimization requirements instead. They were told they could have meaningful work and lifestyle flexibility, but what they received was constant performance pressure with every aspect of life visible for evaluation and comparison. The gap between what was promised and what was experienced created a deep sense of betrayal that was initially internalized as personal inadequacy.

Generation Z represents the first cohort to experience fully algorithmic conditioning from birth. They've never known a world without curated identity pressure and social media comparison. They can recognize system dysfunction more easily than older generations, but they lack frameworks for creating sustainable alternatives because they've never experienced them.

What fascinates me is that Frequency Intelligence provides a common language and practical tools that can be applied across all these groups. It validates the work ethic older generations developed while offering sustainable frameworks. It provides Millennials with the alignment they were promised—delivered through practical implementation tools. It provides Generation Z with systematic approaches that support their natural consciousness while helping them build rather than merely critique existing systems.

Yet across these generational differences, one truth remains: when even one person begins to live differently, the effect ripples outward. This is where transformation begins—not in systems, but in individuals who model another way.

The Transformation
Individual Change Creating Collective Shift

What I've observed repeatedly is how individual shifts in awareness create unexpected changes in the people around them. When someone begins asking different questions about their own timing, energy, and authentic choices, others notice—not because of any deliberate influence, but because authenticity is recognizable and naturally attractive.

I've witnessed how one person's commitment to working from their natural rhythm permits others to question whether chronic urgency is actually necessary. When someone consistently makes decisions based on genuine alignment rather than external pressure, colleagues begin wondering whether they, too, might have choices they hadn't recognized.

Mind you, I've also seen the opposite—how powerful organizational systems can override individual wisdom even when leaders have sincere intentions. The pressure to conform to institutional rhythms often wins, regardless of personal insight or awareness. The transformation, when it happens, occurs not through policy changes or systemic implementation, but through the quiet power of living differently. When people witness that another way of working exists—one that produces strong results while honoring human nature—curiosity emerges naturally.

This is how cultural change actually unfolds—not through top-down declarations or organized movements, but through the accumulation of individual choices to ask different questions and live by different principles. Each person who begins operating from authentic timing and sustainable energy management becomes a quiet demonstration that alternatives to stress-driven achievement are possible.

If these principles can shift organizations, imagine what they can do in our most intimate spaces—parenting, relationships, and family life. The Old System reaches into our homes, too, and so can Frequency Intelligence.

Parenting and Relationship Transformation

The most paradigm-shifting applications of these principles happen in the most intimate settings—how we raise children and navigate close relationships. Many parents realize they unconsciously transmit urgency as a form of love. "Hurry up, we're late." "Don't waste time." "You need to keep up with your peers." The intention is to help children succeed, but what they are actually taught is to override natural rhythm and optimize for external approval.

Parents today operate under tremendous pressure from educational systems and social expectations that equate achievement metrics as evidence of good parenting. But families who begin prioritizing natural developmental timing witness what becomes possible when parenting philosophy shifts from performance optimization to resonance support.

Children in traditional systems are often labeled as having difficulties because they can't maintain focus during lengthy periods, even when they demonstrate exceptional comprehension when information is presented in shorter segments with natural breaks. Rather than adapting to natural learning rhythms, institutions recommend interventions to help children conform to requirements.

However, when these same children transfer to environments that structure learning around natural attention cycles, they demonstrate advanced performance and emotional regulation that never emerged previously. Parents often experience profound relief when they realize how close they came to suppressing their child's natural intelligence in the service of institutional convenience.

What gets systematically excluded from educational foundations is:

Learning to recognize and trust natural energy patterns	Developing the capacity to distinguish between external pressure and genuine internal motivation
Understanding when the body, emotions, or cognitive systems require rest and recalibration instead of continued performance	Making decisions based on timing and alignment rather than fear of falling behind arbitrary schedules

Parents implementing these principles often discover they're raising children who can accurately name their internal phases:

Parents implementing these principles often discover they're raising children who can accurately name their internal phases:

> I'm in a state of focused concentration mode right now

> I'm in reflection phase and need processing time before taking on new learning.

> I feel aligned with this project and want to dedicate creative energy to exploring it.

This isn't permissive parenting—it's resilience education that creates individuals who understand self-regulation, sustainable high performance, and authentic contribution rather than experiencing breakdown in their twenties and thirties.

All of this leads to the heart of the matter: success itself. Because unless we redefine success, the Old System's script will always find its way back into our choices.

A New Definition of Success

At the heart of this transformation is a fundamental redefinition of what success actually means. The Old System measures success through accumulation—more money, more growth, more recognition, more productivity. Frequency Intelligence measures success through emotional imprint—the dynamic alignment between your values and daily choices, your natural capacity and actual commitments, your long-term vision and immediate actions.

This shift changes everything. Instead of optimizing for external metrics that may or may not reflect authentic achievement, you begin optimizing for the subjective experience of sustainable fulfillment. Instead of forcing yourself through arbitrary timelines, you learn to move with timing that honors both individual rhythm and collective needs.

The results often exceed traditional success metrics precisely because they emerge from genuine alignment rather than forced effort. When you build something from your natural frequency, it tends to be more innovative, more sustainable, and more resonant with others who are looking for authentic alternatives to the status quo.

This is the choice point we're all facing, individually and collectively. Do we continue following inherited scripts that optimize for metrics that may not serve human flourishing? Or do we begin asking questions that honor the complexity, creativity, and natural intelligence that make us human?

This redefinition is not abstract—it is lived. My own journey illustrates how these shifts unfold over time, from early awareness to loss, and then to conscious reclamation.

The Choice Point at 41

This is where the personal and the cultural meet. My own life has shown me the cost of following the script—and the liberation that comes from breaking it. At 10, I felt it. At 20, I lost it. At 30, I questioned it again. At 41 and onward, I'm reclaiming it.

That same arc exists collectively: we are all living through the collapse of old scripts that were never composed for human flourishing. We are at the cultural equivalent of 41—the moment of conscious choice. Do we continue following the Old System because it is familiar, or do we reclaim frequency because it is true?

Every person I encounter exists at this choice point. They can continue asking inherited questions focused on external metrics, competitive positioning, and constant optimization—which will likely produce some version of conventional success along with the stress, disconnection, and sustainability challenges that frequently accompany traditional achievement approaches.

Alternatively, they can begin experimenting with questions designed around how consciousness, creativity, and collaboration actually function when supported rather than suppressed. These inquiries open possibilities for forms of success that are more personally satisfying, more environmentally sustainable, and more aligned with authentic individual contribution and collective flourishing.

This choice extends far beyond personal consequences. Every time someone chooses alignment over achievement pressure, natural timing over artificial urgency, collaboration over competitive positioning, they demonstrate through lived example that alternatives exist to the burnout economy, attention fragmentation culture, and chronic stress patterns that many people accept as inevitable.

Individual transformation creates cultural change through social proof—the tendency to adopt behaviors observed in others we respect. When someone demonstrates meaningful success while maintaining health, relationships, and authentic expression, they provide evidence that challenges cultural narratives about necessary sacrifice and inevitable tradeoffs.

Entrepreneurs who build successful businesses using sustainable approaches influence other business owners to question whether growth requires sacrificing personal well-being or team health. Creative professionals who produce outstanding work while honoring natural timing inspire others to experiment with alternatives to forced productivity.

These influences compound over time, creating a cultural momentum that shifts expectations about what is normal and acceptable in terms of approaches to achievement, relationships, and contribution. The transformation occurs through the accumulation of individual choices rather than institutional change, making it more resilient and authentic than top-down cultural initiatives.

The questions you ask yourself shape the reality you create. The intelligence you choose to develop determines not just your individual experience, but the culture you contribute to building.

This is your choice point. This is your moment to reclaim frequency over force, timing over pressure, authentic contribution over extractive productivity.

The Old System is revealing its limitations. Frequency Intelligence offers the alternative.

Choose wisely. The future depends on it.

CHAPTER 7

Beyond Diagnosis
The Intelligence We Never Named

For as long as I can remember, my body has been speaking a language I couldn't translate.

The warm flow through my chest when something felt right. The knot in my stomach when I agreed to the wrong thing. The way my shoulders would ache for weeks when I pushed against resistance. The tears that came, sudden and irrational, when a piece of music or a moment of truth pierced me at the exact frequency my system needed.

I thought this was just being uncomfortable. Too sensitive. Maybe just the way I was built.

For years, I had no words for what my body was doing. I just knew I felt "off" a lot of the time, even when nothing was technically wrong with my life.

I wasn't sick. I didn't have anything diagnosable. I was just … uncomfortable—out of sync. Like I was constantly swimming against some invisible current.

Looking back now, I can see that my body was reading frequency information the entire time. Back then, I had no language for this intelligence, no framework to understand that these sensations were data rather than dysfunction.

My body wasn't broken. It was broadcasting. Every symptom, every wave of fatigue, every sleepless night was not an error in my design. It was information.

For years, I misread those signals. Instead of listening, I overrode them. I drank more coffee, worked longer hours, and doubled down on discipline. I told myself I needed to keep up. If I could only manage this period better, I'd be fine. If I meditated harder, pushed harder, and achieved more, eventually the dissonance would resolve.

It never did.

What I understand now is that my body was not the problem. My body was the intelligence system I had ignored all along.

After building FQ and listening to people in my coaching, I've realized I wasn't alone, and I was misreading the signals. What I was feeling wasn't weakness. It was information.

Looking back through the FQ lens, I can see that for over a decade, I've been trapped in a forced Launch cycle— forcing myself to do more, be better, and achieve greater effectiveness and success. My body was telling me about its resistance to this misalignment the entire time, but I didn't have the knowledge or language to understand.

This is the part of human intelligence that has never been named, measured, or systematically developed. The intelligence that doesn't come from thinking (IQ) or relating (EQ), but from reading energy, timing, and rhythm. The capacity to detect alignment and misalignment in real time.

I call it Frequency Intelligence.

FQ complements medicine and therapy; it does not replace them. Many conditions require diagnosis and treatment. This chapter focuses on the frequency layer that is often ignored but can prevent collapse when addressed.

What I've realized—through many hours of working with individuals, through my own journey of misalignment and coherence—is that most of what we call "disorders" are often signals from this intelligence. Signals we've misinterpreted, medicalized, or pathologized—simply because we didn't know them as intelligence at all.

The Pattern Hidden in 40,000 Hours

I've worked with hundreds of people, helping them describe their struggles. Leaders, artists, parents, students. High achievers and those who felt perpetually behind. Across industries, cultures, and generations.

Their words varied, but the essence was strikingly similar:

I feel exhausted, but I don't know why. On paper, my life appears to be going well, but inside, it feels off. I can't focus, no matter how hard I try. I don't feel like myself anymore.

Some carried diagnoses: anxiety, depression, ADHD, autism, autoimmune disorders, chronic fatigue, and fibromyalgia. Others had no diagnosis at all but felt just as lost.

For years, I accepted these as separate conditions requiring various treatments. Eventually, after 40,000 hours of observation, I began to see something no one else was seeing: despite the different labels, the energetic signature was identical.

Their bodies were tightening, resisting, slowing down. Their energy was fragmented, scattered, drained. Their minds were foggy or racing, unable to find balance. Their emotions were heavy, flat, or explosive.

No matter what diagnosis was attached—or whether there was a diagnosis at all—the underlying pattern was the same. They were all operating out of sync with their natural frequency.

This realization changed everything. What if depression, anxiety, ADHD, and chronic fatigue weren't fundamentally separate conditions? What if they were different manifestations of the same phenomenon: the breakdown that occurs when we live against our Frequency Intelligence?

Looking back through the lens I've since developed, I can see patterns that weren't visible at the time.

I remember working with different individuals who described "losing their edge"—feeling flat, unmotivated, like they were "phoning it in" at work. Their doctors suggested antidepressants. Their therapists explored childhood trauma. Yet when I traced their energy patterns, a different picture emerged: eighteen months of constant Launch mode. No breaks. No reflection time.

No periods of restoration. Their systems weren't depressed—they appeared depleted from living against natural rhythms.

I worked with creative professionals who couldn't focus and had been diagnosed with adult ADHD. Yet their patterns suggested something else: they were trying to force deep creative work during natural low-energy times while scheduling meetings during peak creative hours. The focus issues seemed to map more closely to timing misalignment than attention disorders.

I saw leaders with what they called "chronic anxiety"—panic attacks multiple times per week, considering leaving their jobs. In those cases, their lifestyles revealed chronic nervous system overwhelm: too much caffeine, constant phone checking, too little sleep, absorbing everyone else's emotional states. Their anxiety appeared to be an appropriate response to chronic frequency disruption rather than a disorder.

These patterns—the gap between diagnostic labels and energetic reality—became the foundation for what I would later develop as Frequency Intelligence. I began to see that much of what we medicalize might actually be the body's intelligent response to misaligned living.

The issue isn't that people are broken—it's that they're living in ways that break their natural frequency. Since our culture only has diagnostic language for these experiences, everyone assumes they need fixing rather than realigning.

Frequency misalignment appears to be indisputably preventable. Because no one understood this pattern before, people suffered through years of symptoms, treatments, and labels for what could potentially have been resolved through Frequency Intelligence from the start.

Why Frequency Has Been Culturally Invisible

If this intelligence is so obvious once you see it, why has it taken us this long to recognize it?

We didn't have language for it. Western culture has words for intellect (IQ) and emotion (EQ), but not for frequency. We can describe thought and feeling, but not alignment. Without language, signals get misfiled.

Medicine is calibrated for crisis. The medical system excels at identifying pathology and treating acute breakdown. It was never intended to recognize early misalignment or cyclical rhythm. So when people show signs of dissonance, we label them as disordered—rather than misaligned.

Our culture only recognizes two states: functional or dysfunctional. If you're meeting society's demands, you're "healthy." If you're not, you're "sick." There's no middle category for out of rhythm. We are witnessing the rise of diagnosis as identity. Especially in the last decade, diagnosis has become more than a medical tool—it's become a cultural marker. People find relief in naming their struggle, but then build identities around the labels. What could have been a temporary signal becomes a permanent self-concept.

We've normalized the ache. The invisible exhaustion of misalignment is now considered the new baseline—coffee to function, medication to sleep, apps to focus. We treat constant struggle as the baseline of modern life, rather than asking why.

FQ has remained invisible because we weren't looking for it. We assumed breakdown was failure rather than feedback. We mistook the body's signals as betrayal rather than guidance.

Only now—through pattern recognition, through the epidemic of diagnosis, through the sheer unsustainability of modern systems—have I been able to name what's actually happening.

The Language Gap

Think about the words we use for human experience. We have extensive vocabulary for dysfunction: anxiety, depression, burnout, ADHD, OCD, trauma, and disorder.

Where is our vocabulary for alignment? For coherence? For resonance? For timing?

Without that vocabulary, we collapse everything into the language of illness.

A student who can't sit still in a classroom becomes ADHD. An executive who loses motivation becomes depressed. A sensitive person in a chaotic office becomes anxious. A parent who feels depleted becomes burned out.

This is how behavior becomes identity.

What if these weren't illnesses at all? What if they were frequency signals—accurate, intelligent responses to misaligned environments?

Without the language of frequency, we misinterpret intelligence as pathology. We medicate what we should be listening to. We suppress what we should be decoding.

This is why I believe Frequency Intelligence represents not just a personal insight but a cultural breakthrough. It gives us words for an intelligence that has always existed but has never been named or used.

The Language Revolution
Making the Invisible Visible

Language doesn't just describe reality—it creates it. For decades, we've had hundreds of words for dysfunction and almost none for optimal functioning. This linguistic imbalance has shaped how we see ourselves and each other.

Frequency Intelligence represents more than new vocabulary—it's a fundamental reframe of human potential. When someone can say "I'm in a Reflect phase" instead of "I'm depressed," when they can identify "environmental overstimulation" instead of "anxiety," they immediately move from patient to participant, from broken to broadcasting.

This language revolution will be quiet but irreversible. Children will grow up with frequency literacy as natural as emotional vocabulary. They'll learn to read their energy patterns alongside reading books. They'll understand that their sensitivity is information, not dysfunction, that their attention moves in cycles, not deficits.

Workplace cultures will shift from managing burnout to preventing it, from accommodating differences to leveraging them for growth and innovation. Healthcare will expand from treating symptoms to supporting alignment. Education will evolve from forcing compliance to honoring rhythm.

The moment we have precise language for what we're experiencing, we gain power over it. Frequency intelligence gives us that precision—and that power.

The Science We Ignored

What I call Frequency Intelligence isn't mystical—it operationalizes what research has been showing us for decades. We had the data; we just didn't have the framework to connect it.

Circadian and Ultradian Rhythms: Research reveals that humans operate on multiple biological clocks. Our circadian rhythm governs our 24-hour cycle of alertness and rest. But equally important are ultradian rhythms—90 to 120-minute cycles of peak attention followed by natural restoration periods. Most workplaces ignore these entirely, expecting sustained focus for eight hours straight.

Heart Rate Variability and Coherence: Studies show that emotional states directly affect heart rhythm patterns. When we're stressed or misaligned, our heart rate becomes erratic. When we're in flow or coherence, it becomes smooth and organized. This isn't metaphor—it's measurable physiology that validates what frequency practitioners intuitively know.

Attention Restoration Theory: Research in environmental psychology demonstrates that our cognitive capacity is finite and requires specific types of restoration. Natural environments, quiet spaces, and reduced stimulation aren't luxuries—they're neurological necessities for sustained performance.

Sensory Processing and Overstimulation: Neuroscience confirms that individuals have dramatically different thresholds for sensory input. What one person experiences as energizing stimulation, another experiences as overwhelming noise. Yet our environments are designed as if everyone processes information identically.

Chronotype Research: Studies on individual timing preferences show that people have genetic variations in their optimal sleep and wake times. Some are naturally early risers, while others are night owls. Forcing everyone into the same schedule isn't just inefficient—it's working against biology.

Polyvagal Theory: Research on the autonomic nervous system reveals that we have different states of activation—social engagement, fight-or-flight, and shutdown. Our environments and interactions constantly shift us between these states, yet we rarely design with this in mind.

The tragedy is that this research sits in academic journals while people suffer from misalignment in the real world. What I've done with FQ is create a practical framework that bridges this gap—translating scientific insights into daily applications.

We don't need more research to prove that humans are rhythmic beings. We need frameworks to honor what we already know.

From Trauma as Currency to Frequency as Guidance

Into this vacuum of language, something else has emerged: trauma as symbolic capital.

In the last decade, pain has become performance. Vulnerability has become a marketing strategy. Book deals, speaking gigs, social media platforms—all increasingly give rise to on stories of breakdown and recovery.

I've watched this dynamic unfold with fascination and discomfort. On one hand, it's liberating that people can finally share their struggles without shame. On the other hand, it creates a distorted incentive: pain becomes permission.

The more dramatic your suffering, the more legitimate your voice. The deeper your trauma, the greater your platform.

This isn't a conspiracy; it's conditioning—shaped by algorithms that reward emotional engagement and by cultures that crave dramatic transformation arcs.

Oddly, the effect is massive: people unconsciously attach to their pain because it brings recognition, a sense of belonging, and sometimes financial reward. Healing becomes threatening because it means losing the identity and community built around struggle.

Here's the paradox: trauma culture validates struggle but doesn't resolve it. It explains breakdown, but doesn't teach self-awareness. It celebrates survival but doesn't teach sustainability.

FQ offers a way out. Instead of asking, "What broke you?" it asks, "What's your rhythm now?" Instead of defaulting to collapse, it invites you to prevent it. Instead of building identity around wounds, it builds agency around signals.

This is pro-coherence. It's about restoring the missing language so we can recognize that pain is information about alignment, not just pathology.

The Algorithm of Pain

Social media amplifies this dynamic: algorithms reward drama, conflict, and high emotional charge. Struggle gets more engagement than peace. Breakdown gets more views than breakthrough.

So we are trained, subtly but powerfully: Document your wounds. Amplify your pain. Stay raw for relevance.

Pain becomes permission.

The irony is painful: the very platforms that could spread wisdom are training us to remain in misalignment because pain is more profitable than peace.

The Digital Algorithm of Dysfunction

The platforms we constructed to connect us have become the primary training grounds for frequency disruption. However, the damage goes far past distraction: social media has fundamentally rewired our relationship with pain and power.

Over the past fifteen years, digital environments have created unprecedented conditions that systematically fragment human attention and overstimulate nervous systems, which have evolved for much smaller tribal environments. The average person checks their phone every six minutes, training their brain to scatter rather than focus. Constant exposure to curated highlight reels triggers chronic inadequacy responses that human psychology never evolved to handle.

In practice, the most insidious effect is how algorithms reward emotional intensity over wisdom, crisis over connection, breakdown over breakthrough. The platforms that could spread Frequency Intelligence instead amplify frequency disruption—because dysfunction generates more engagement than alignment.

Social media has trained entire generations to perform their pain for attention, to monetize their struggles before healing them, to build platforms on wounds rather than wisdom. Young people learn that their value comes from their trauma rather than their capacity for creation.

When Frequency Intelligence becomes mainstream, this will reverse. Platforms will begin rewarding coherence, presence, and sustainable success rather than dramatic collapse and recovery cycles. The algorithm will finally serve human thriving rather than human addiction.

The Economic Revolution
From Extraction to Regeneration

We've established an economy that depends on human depletion. The current system requires people to override their signals, ignore their rhythms, and sacrifice their sustainability for productivity. This creates massive secondary markets—coffee shops on every corner because people need stimulants to function, meditation apps because minds are too scattered to focus naturally, and pharmaceuticals because nervous systems are too activated to rest.

The trauma economy represents the latest evolution of this extraction model. Pain becomes capital. Breakdown becomes brand. Recovery becomes content. People unconsciously remain attached to their struggles because those struggles generate recognition, community, and sometimes financial reward.

To reframe, Frequency Intelligence threatens this entire structure. When people learn to prevent breakdown rather than monetize it, when they design for integration rather than collapse, the extraction economy becomes obsolete.

Organizations that master frequency stewardship will have enormous competitive advantages—not through burning people out faster, but through sustaining human energy longer. They'll attract the most talented people because those people will be able to do their best work without sacrificing their health.

The shift from trauma economy to frequency economy will be one of the most significant cultural transformations of our time. Success will be measured not by how much suffering you can survive, but by how much suffering you can prevent. Wealth will flow to those who can create without extraction, lead without depletion, and innovate without breakdown.

The Day I Chose Silence

There was a time when I could have easily joined this economy. I had the story: the heartbreak, the investor rejection, the collapse, the private grief. The arc was perfect.

In any case, when I considered sharing it in real time, my body gave me the same clear message it always had: resistance.

Something in me knew that if I led with my breakdown, I would build an audience addicted to breakdown. If I made trauma my teaching credential, I would create a community organized around wounds, not wisdom.

So I chose differently. I chose silence. Integration. Private healing. This choice cost me influence and relevance, but it preserved something more important: my frequency.

Because this I knew: if I spoke before my signal was clear, I would just be feeding the very cycle I came to transform.

Beyond Performance, Beyond Pathology

When I finally began listening differently, I saw the truth: My body was not weak. It was wise. My resistance was not failure. It was information. My fatigue was not laziness. It was timing.

This was not something medicine had taught me. It was not something I read in a leadership manual or self-help book. It was a discovery born from paying attention to the pattern beneath thousands of conversations and my own lived experience.

Once I saw it, I couldn't unsee it.

We are not just thinking beings (IQ) or feeling beings (EQ). We are rhythmic, energetic beings (FQ). Our intelligence is not limited to cognition and emotion. It extends to frequency.

The future of human sustainability depends on whether we learn to develop this intelligence.

Without it, we will keep pathologizing signals as disorders, monetizing trauma as capital, and mistaking collapse for the only route to transformation.

With it, we can begin to see misalignment as signal, resistance as guidance, and resonance as strategy.

When Misalignment Gets Medicalized

I want to be clear: diagnosis has its place.

For many, it is lifesaving. It offers language when silence feels suffocating. It provides legitimacy when you've been gaslit by culture or family. It opens doors to treatment, accommodation, and understanding. I would never argue against that.

Truth be told, diagnosis has also become our only lens. The sole way we know how to explain struggle. If you cannot keep up with society's pace, the assumption is that the problem must be you. If your body refuses the system's rhythm, you are sick. If your nervous system collapses, you are disordered.

We don't have vocabulary for misalignment. We don't treat dissonance as wisdom. We don't recognize resistance as guidance. Instead, we label, medicate, and return people to the same misaligned systems that broke them in the first place.

From Signal to Symptom Here's how it plays out:

A student who struggles to sit still in class is diagnosed with ADHD. Perhaps their system is accurately signaling that eight hours of forced attention in artificial light is a mismatch for human development.

An executive who loses motivation is diagnosed with depression. Perhaps their system is signaling that eighteen months of nonstop output with no Reflect phase is unsustainable.

A parent who feels anxious is diagnosed with generalized anxiety disorder. Perhaps their system is signaling chronic overstimulation—coffee, screens, sleep debt, emotional caretaking with no restoration.

In each case, the signals are valid. Instead of asking what they mean, we pathologize them. Instead of treating misalignment, we treat the person as broken.

This is not to deny the reality of clinical conditions. Some people do live with profound neurological differences or biochemical imbalances. But many more are being mislabeled—not because they are sick, but because their environment is.

The Rise of Diagnosis as Identity

In recent years, diagnosis has become more than medical. It has become identity.

I hear it constantly:

I have anxiety. *I'm ADHD. I'm in survival mode. I'm neurodivergent. I'm traumatized. I'm stressed. I have depression.*

There is relief in naming your struggle, though there is danger in building your selfhood around it.

The shift from "I am experiencing anxiety" to "I am an anxious person" may seem small, but it transforms a temporary state into a permanent identity.

Once diagnosis becomes identity, here's what unfolds:

You become invested in the label. Your community, credibility, and even livelihood may form around it, eventually depending on it. You stop asking more veiled questions. Instead of exploring patterns of misalignment, you focus on managing the disorder. You lose agency. The diagnosis positions you as a patient, not a participant. You miss the intelligence. You interpret what your system is broadcasting as failure rather than guidance.

This is not empowerment. It is entrapment.

Diagnosis should be a description, not a definition—a tool, not a totality. Unfortunately, in our culture, it has become the main stage upon which people perform their legitimacy.

Frequency as Missing Language

If diagnosis gives us names, frequency gives us navigational coordinates.

This is where Frequency Intelligence enters as something bigger than medicine, psychology, or self-help. It does not compete with diagnosis; it completes the picture. It offers the missing language. Instead of asking, *What disorder explains this?* these are the questions it asks:

What is the frequency state of this person? Are they in resonance or dissonance? Are they forcing action in a Reflect season, or resting during a Launch season? Is the nervous system showing breakdown, or is it signaling misalignment with timing?

These are not fluffy questions. They are strategic. They reframe the human being not as a machine that sometimes fails, but as a cyclical, energetic system that must be read and led with the same intelligence we apply to sustainable economies or resilient ecosystems.

Frequency language changes everything because it restores agency. Instead of being someone who "has" a condition, you become someone who is experiencing a state. Instead of being limited by your diagnosis, you become empowered by your self-knowledge.

When someone understands that their afternoon energy crash is not due to ADHD but rather a natural part of their circadian rhythm, they can design their day differently. When someone recognizes that their seasonal depression is not a pathology but an honest response to a lack of light and increased introspection needs, they can prepare for and work with these cycles.

When someone sees that their sensitivity to crowds is not social anxiety but energetic overwhelm, they can create strategies for protection and restoration rather than avoidance and medication.

Frequency language gives us precision, whereas diagnosis offers us categories. It provides us movement where labels give us stasis. It gives us agency where pathology gives us powerlessness.

When someone says, "I have anxiety," the conversation typically ends with treatment options. When someone says, "My system is overstimulated and needs recalibration," the conversation begins with practical steps toward alignment.

40,000 Hours of Listening

In my almost twenty years of working with individuals over 40,000 hours of listening at every stage of life, I've witnessed this pattern repeatedly.

People collapse into "burnout," not because they lack resilience, but because they've been trapped in Launch cycles for years without ever entering Reflect.

People are labeled as anxious when, in fact, their energy appears to be vibrating ahead of the pace their environment can recognize.

People are called depressive when what they're really experiencing might be the necessary stillness of a deep Reflect phase.

People whose nervous systems reject constant urgency, but who are medicated so they can continue functioning in systems that were never sustainable, are not broken—they're responding appropriately to broken environments.

Again and again, I see the same truth: the body isn't betraying us. It's communicating.

When We Can't Find Our Frequency, We Attach to Our Pain

This is what I see happening beneath the surface: People are desperate to be seen, but unsure how to show up without their pain as proof.

It's not because they're weak. It's because we've given them no other language. In a world that equates visibility with trauma and identity with pathology, pain becomes the only place to be real.

This attachment to pain serves several unconscious functions:

- It explains why life feels hard. Instead of having to examine whether your choices are aligned with your nature, you can point to your diagnosis as the reason things are difficult.

- It provides community. Diagnosis creates an instant sense of belonging with others who share your label. You find your tribe through shared struggle rather than shared values or vision.

- It generates sympathy. Pain makes people want to help you, support you, and give you special consideration. It becomes a form of social protection.

- It excuses limitation. When you "have" a condition, you're not expected to push beyond it. You can point to your diagnosis as the reason you can't do certain things.

- It creates purpose. Many people find meaning in their struggle. They become advocates for their condition, teachers about their trauma, and inspirations through their survival.

- None of these functions is inherently wrong. But they become problematic when they keep people attached to identities of limitation rather than identities of possibility.

- The real tragedy is that people become so invested in these secondary benefits of pain that they resist the primary benefit of healing: freedom.

FQ Is Not Another Healing System

This isn't anti-care—it's pro-coherence.

Frequency Intelligence isn't about fixing what's wrong with you. It's about teaching you to speak from your alignment rather than your injury. To make decisions from your rhythm, not your triggers. To learn the timing of your energy, not just the history of your trauma.

Where most systems ask: *What happened to you? What do you need to heal?*

FQ asks: *Where are you in your energetic cycle? What's the cleanest next move from here?*

It's not that healing isn't relevant. It's just not the whole map.

The healing industry, despite its good intentions, has created its own form of dependency. People spend years, sometimes decades, processing their past without ever learning how to navigate their present. They become experts in their trauma but strangers to their power.

They can tell you in detail about their childhood wounds, their relationship patterns, their triggers, and traumas. But they can't tell you when they have the most energy, what environments help them thrive, or how to design their days for sustainable success.

FQ doesn't dismiss therapeutic work, but it doesn't require you to live in the past to understand the present. It meets you where you are now and asks: *What does your energy need to move forward from this moment?*

This shift is profound because it restores sovereignty. Instead of waiting to be fixed by others, you learn to read and respond to your own signals. Instead of seeking permission from professionals, you develop trust in your own intelligence. Instead of remaining dependent on external validation, you cultivate internal authority.

You're Not in a Diagnosis You're in a Pattern

The question is no longer *what's wrong with me?* but *what timing am I in?*

FQ Reframes: From Pathology to Pattern

FQ replaces the language of "what's wrong with me?" with the language of frequency patterns:

- I'm burned out. → I've been in output too long.

- I have anxiety. → My system's overstimulated.

- I'm overwhelmed. → I'm out of sync and absorbing too much.

- I'm lazy. → I'm in a Reflect phase and not meant to be producing right now.

- I can't focus. → My attention is scattered—I need to recenter.

- I'm stressed. → I'm moving faster than my nervous system can sustain.

- I'm depressed. → I'm in deep processing and need to honor this timing.

- I have insomnia. → My mind is overstimulated and needs deeper rest preparation.

- I'm procrastinating. → My energy is resisting forced motion. I need to realign.

- I'm unmotivated. → I'm not aligned with what I'm being asked to do.

Additional common reframes:

- I'm stuck. → I'm in transition—clarity hasn't yet arrived.

- I feel lost. → I'm between cycles—my new direction is still forming.

- I'm exhausted. → I've overridden my natural rhythm—I need restoration.

- I'm failing. → My current strategy isn't aligned—I need to adjust my timing.

- I'm insecure. → I've lost coherence—I need to return to my baseline frequency.

- I'm indecisive. → It's not time to choose yet—the frequency isn't clear.

This isn't self-help fluff. It's precision language for an energetic world. It restores agency. It invites rhythm. It honors timing. And it helps you lead—without performing suffering first.

When you shift from diagnostic language to frequency language, everything changes:

You stop seeing "broken" and start seeing "temporarily misaligned." You stop waiting for treatment and start making adjustments. You stop identifying with your struggles and start identifying with your capacity for alignment. You stop being a victim of your circumstances and start being a steward of your frequency. You stop looking for someone to fix you and start learning how to tune yourself.

This shift doesn't happen overnight. After years or decades of thinking in diagnostic terms, it takes time to develop frequency literacy. Even so, the change in perspective can be immediate—and immediately empowering.

The Structural Roots of Collapse

Here's the truth: individual suffering is real, but much of it is structural.

You cannot look at rising rates of anxiety, depression, and burnout without also looking at the systems people are forced to live inside.

Work rhythms are designed for machines, not humans. Education systems are built for compliance rather than for fostering curiosity.

Digital environments overload nervous systems. Social norms reward visibility over intentional unity. Urban life separates us from nature, light, and silence.

Is it any wonder people collapse? What is remarkable is that so many still manage to function at all.

When we treat each case as an isolated medical problem, we miss the larger truth: these symptoms are predictable outcomes of systemic misalignment.

This is where Frequency Intelligence offers a radical shift. It asks us to see signals as data, not dysfunction. To interpret resistance as guidance, not betrayal. To recognize that collapse is not inevitable—it is preventable when we learn to design for alignment.

Generational Signals Collapse as the New Normal

When I look back over nearly two decades of listening, I see something striking: every generation has been negotiating with frequency misalignment in its own way.

The stories sound different, the labels change, the environments shift—but beneath it all, the pattern is the same. Human beings are living out of rhythm with themselves, and each generation has invented its own explanation for why this is the case.

The body has been broadcasting the signals for decades, but we did not have the words. We did not have a framework. We did not know. Frequency Intelligence hadn't been discovered yet. That's why this intelligence has remained invisible—not because people were blind, but because they lacked the concept to interpret what they were experiencing.

What people did have were cultural scripts, and those scripts shaped how they responded to their signals.

Boomers and Gen X Endurance as Virtue

For Boomers and Gen X, the dominant message was push through. If you were exhausted, you worked harder. If you were unhappy, you endured. If you were struggling, you kept it private.

The body wasn't a source of intelligence; it was a problem to discipline. The nervous system wasn't an ally; it was something to override. Rest was often framed as laziness, sensitivity was viewed as weakness, and boundaries were perceived as selfishness.

I've sat across from countless individuals in their 50s and 60s who have achieved extraordinary careers, raised families, and accumulated wealth—all while ignoring the quiet signals of misalignment. Their reward was social legitimacy. Their cost was deferred breakdown.

Stress became hypertension. Suppressed emotions became depression. Overridden exhaustion became chronic fatigue or autoimmune conditions. Many reached their later years with money in the bank but energy bankrupt.

They never learned frequency literacy. They never had the language to see their body's refusal as wisdom. So, their struggles were medicalized: diabetes, hypertension, burnout, and chronic pain.

The tragedy is that much of this could have been prevented if they'd been taught to honor rhythm instead of overriding it.

Millennials—Naming the Ache

Millennials came of age in a different environment. Therapy became mainstream. Talking about stress and burnout became socially acceptable. Diagnosis culture expanded, and suddenly there was language—perhaps too much—to describe inner struggle.

For the first time, it was permissible to say, *I'm anxious, I'm depressed,* or *I'm burned out.* This was revolutionary compared to the silence of previous generations.

Beneath it all, the language itself carried a trap. Instead of frequency signals being interpreted as guidance, they were pathologized. Instead of seeing misalignment as a natural response to unsustainable conditions, it became framed as personal disorder. I remember one millennial telling me, "It feels like my whole generation was born tired." Another said, "We were told we could be anything, but no one told us how to sustain being anything."

Millennials became experts in naming their struggles—burnout, anxiety, trauma, depression—but often remained trapped inside those labels. They processed endlessly, sought therapies, tried wellness programs, but without frequency literacy, they lacked the tools to prevent breakdown before it happened.

They were also the first generation to fall unavoidably into the algorithm of pain. Social media rewarded vulnerability as performance. Breakdown became content. Pain became proof of authenticity. Many millennials erected platforms on their wounds before they had even had the chance to integrate them.

They didn't mean to perform. They were reflexively responding to cultural cues. The net result was a generation carrying layered wisdom without the frameworks to apply it sustainably.

Gen Z–Diagnosis as Identity

Gen Z inherited an entirely new landscape. Mental health terms are native to their vocabulary. They say "I have anxiety" with the same casualness that earlier generations might have said "I have a cold."

On one hand, this destigmatization is a victory. Young people are seeking help earlier. They're talking about their struggles openly. They're not carrying shame in the same way their parents and grandparents did.

There's also a shadow: for many, diagnosis has become identity. Instead of describing temporary states, labels become permanent self-concepts. *I am anxious. I am neurodivergent. I am traumatized.*

This shift collapses possibility. What could have been a signal becomes a fixed identity. What could have been recalibration becomes lifelong pathology.

Because Gen Z has grown up fully immersed in performative culture, their pain is personal and public. Every breakdown can be documented, every struggle live-streamed, every flare-up turned into content. The boundary between authentic self-expression and algorithm-driven performance is nearly impossible to navigate.

This has created a paradox: a generation that is more attuned to mental health than any before, but also more fragile, overstimulated, and misaligned. They don't lack language—they lack frequency literacy. They know how to name what's wrong, but not how to align with what's right.

Generation Alpha Canaries in the Coal Mine

The youngest generation, those born after 2010, is already showing even more dramatic responses to frequency disruption: rising rates of childhood anxiety, ADHD diagnoses, sensory processing issues, and behavioral challenges.

From a traditional perspective, these trends are alarming. From a frequency perspective, they are entirely predictable. Children's systems are highly sensitive. They haven't learned to override their signals. So when placed in environments of chronic misalignment, digital overstimulation, rigid schooling structures, and parental burnout, they respond immediately and visibly.

They aren't broken. They're responding. They are showing us what happens when human beings are raised in environments that ignore natural rhythm.

The Educational Transformation
Raising Frequency-Native Humans

Imagine educational systems conceptualized around human development rather than administrative convenience. Schools that honor different chronotypes instead of forcing all children into identical schedules. We need learning environments that adapt to individual sensitivity levels rather than overwhelming sensory-sensitive children while under-stimulating those who need more input.

Children learn to say "I need movement to think clearly" instead of being diagnosed with ADHD. Young people understand "I process information deeply" instead of being labeled as learning disabled. Students recognize "I'm in a reflection phase" instead of being told they're unmotivated.

This transformation doesn't require massive funding or technology overhauls. It requires recognizing that children are energetic beings with natural rhythms, not production units that should function identically.

The first schools to implement frequency-aware education will produce graduates with unprecedented capabilities. It won't be because they're more intelligent. It will be because they learned to work with their intelligence rather than against it. These students will become the leaders who transform every industry they enter.

Collapse as the New Normal

Taken together, these generational patterns reveal a startling truth: breakdown has become normalized.

For Boomers and Gen X, breakdown typically occurs late in life after decades of endurance. For Millennials, breakdown tends to appear around midlife—often named as burnout or described as emotional collapse. For Gen Z, breakdown arrives almost immediately, framed as identity from adolescence. For Generation Alpha, breakdown begins in childhood.

Each generation breaks down sooner because they are living in more frequency-disrupted conditions. Because we still lack the language of frequency, we continue to treat breakdown as pathology rather than a failure of prevention.

This is why diagnosis rates climb decade after decade. Not necessarily because humans are weaker, but because environments are harsher, rhythms are more ignored, and frequency misalignment is more intense than ever.

We are witnessing a cultural tipping point. Human beings are signaling en masse that the systems we've constructed—educational, economic, and organizational—are unsustainable. Yet instead of listening, we keep trying to medicate the signals away.

The Generational Bridge
From Trauma Currency to Frequency Literacy

Each generation has carried a piece of this puzzle. Boomers and Gen X learned to override their signals—their bodies are now collecting the debt. Millennials learned to name their struggles but often remained trapped in diagnostic identities. Gen Z grew up in a diagnosis culture, speaking mental health casually but risking collapse into limiting labels.

Generation Alpha represents the first opportunity to grow up with frequency literacy from the beginning. They could learn to trust their signals while developing their minds and design their lives around a sustainable rhythm rather than having to recover Frequency Intelligence later.

Nonetheless, this requires the older generations to model a different way. To stop rewarding pain performance and start celebrating quiet coherence. To shift from "push through" to "pause and calibrate." To move from trauma as credential to alignment as authority.

The bridge between trauma culture and frequency culture is being manifested by individuals who choose presence over performance, who refuse to monetize their pain before healing it, and who demonstrate that sustainable power is more valuable than dramatic survival.

Leadership in the Age of Frequency

Leaders don't just set the pace. They set nervous systems.

This has profound implications for leadership, as leaders are not only responsible for their own alignment—they also influence entire ecosystems.

I have worked with leaders who were celebrated publicly but were privately unraveling. They carried enormous pressure, holding together teams and organizations while silently collapsing inside. They had diagnostic words for what they were experiencing: stress, exhaustion, and anxiety. Yet they didn't have a strategy for leading differently.

These leaders often felt trapped. They knew their pace was unsustainable, but they didn't know how to slow down without disappointing others. They knew their stress was affecting their teams, but they didn't know how to model something different. They knew they needed change, but they didn't have frameworks for change that didn't involve crises.

I worked with a woman who was celebrated as a visionary leader. Her company was growing rapidly, her team was loyal, and her investors were thrilled. Despite that, she was secretly having panic attacks before every board meeting. She was taking sleep medication because her mind wouldn't stop racing. She was drinking every night to calm her nervous system.

She had tried therapy. She had tried meditation. She had tried delegation, time management, and boundary setting. Nothing worked because she was trying to fix herself rather than align herself with her true nature.

Looking back through the frequency lens I've since developed, I can see what was happening. She was trapped in constant Launch mode with no natural rhythm of restoration. Her panic wasn't pathology—it was her system signaling chronic misalignment.

What she needed wasn't more therapy or better time management. She needed to honor natural cycles of energy, to recognize when her nervous system required restoration, to lead from rhythm rather than force.

This pattern—and the gap between what leaders actually need and what they're offered—is what led me to develop FQ as a framework. I saw the same energetic signature across different clients: brilliant people breaking themselves against systems that ignored human rhythm.

Productivity won't decrease—it will increase. Creativity won't suffer—it will flourish. Team retention won't decline—it will improve. Because when people work from alignment rather than force, they produce better results with less effort.

Frequency Intelligence gives leaders this strategy. It shows them that leadership doesn't have to mean constant urgency. The nervous system is not a liability, but an instrument. Rhythm, resonance, and rest are not signs of weakness but indicators of sustainability.

When leaders embody this, teams change. Urgency decreases. Creativity rises. Retention improves. Not because of motivational speeches, but because alignment is contagious. People can feel when someone is living in vibrational rapport—it gives them permission to do the same.

Leadership as Frequency Stewardship

Leaders of the Old System are managers of force. They coordinate resources, maximize output, push people harder, and drive toward outcomes regardless of cost. Their success is measured by what they extract from their teams, their organizations, and their markets.

Leaders of the New System will be stewards of frequency. They will learn to feel timing in their organizations. They will design rhythms that honor human energy cycles. They will understand that rest is not wasted time, but the precondition for creativity and sustainable performance.

This is not soft. This is strategic. A company aligned with frequency will outlast, out-innovate, and outperform competitors who burn through their people. A society aligned with frequency will produce citizens who are healthier, more resilient, and better equipped to solve the crises we face.

The companies that understand this will win in the future. They'll be the ones with low turnover, high creativity, and sustainable growth. They'll be the ones that attract the best talent and keep them. They'll be the ones that innovate rather than imitate, that lead rather than react.

This shift requires leaders who have done their own frequency work. You cannot steward what you do not understand. You cannot guide others to alignment if you are living in misalignment yourself. You cannot create sustainable systems if you are operating from unsustainable patterns.

The new leadership development will not be about building better strategies or stronger disciplines. It will be about cultivating Frequency Intelligence. Teaching leaders how to read energy—their own and others'. How to design for rhythm rather than resistance. How to create cultures of coherence rather than chaos.

Frequency stewardship means understanding that every decision you make affects the collective nervous system. Every meeting you schedule, every deadline you set, and every expectation you create either supports or undermines the frequency of your organization.

Leaders who understand this become healers in the most heartfelt and elemental sense. Not because they fix broken people, but because they create conditions that allow people to function optimally. Not because they manage dysfunction, but because they design for field fidelity.

Designing Organizations for Frequency

What does it look like to build companies around human rhythm rather than mechanical efficiency? It requires rethinking everything from meeting design to office architecture.

Meeting Redesign. Most meetings are frequency destroyers—too long, poorly timed, energy-draining. Frequency-aware meetings are shorter (forty-five minutes maximum), scheduled during collective peak windows, and designed with clear outcomes. Teams map their energy patterns and protect individual peak times for deep work.

Energy-Aware Scheduling. Instead of forcing uniform eight-hour days, organizations can implement rhythmic calendaring. Team members declare their Peak, Steady, and Low energy windows. Deep creative work gets Peak time; administrative tasks land in Low periods. Meetings occur during Steady windows when people can engage but aren't sacrificing their most valuable cognitive hours.

Environment by Function. Frequency intelligence recognizes that different work requires different environments. Quiet zones for focused thinking, collaborative spaces for ideation, transition areas for decompression. The physical architecture supports rather than fights human neurology.

Restoration as Strategy. High-performing teams build restoration into their workflow. This isn't "wellness" as an add-on. It's an operational necessity: regular breaks, walking meetings, device-free hours, and seasonal sprint patterns that include formal reflection weeks.

Energy Budgets. Teams start treating attention like the finite resource it is. Projects receive energy budgets alongside time and cost budgets. When teams approach their attention capacity, they pause and recalibrate rather than pushing through to breakdown. The companies implementing these principles aren't becoming softer—they're becoming more precise. They're winning through alignment rather than force.

The Leadership Evolution From Force to Frequency

Leadership is evolving from commanding compliance to stewarding calibration. Leaders who master Frequency Intelligence will dramatically outperform those who continue to operate from force-based models.

Traditional leadership extracts energy until collapse. Leaders work longer hours than their teams, model urgency as virtue, and measure success by short-term output regardless of long-term sustainability.

Frequency leadership regenerates energy through alignment. These leaders understand their own rhythms and tailor their leadership style around them. They recognize their role as nervous system regulators, not just taskmasters. They create cultures where people can do their best work without sacrificing their health.

This isn't softer leadership—it's more precise leadership. When teams work from alignment rather than force, they innovate faster, make better decisions, and sustain higher performance over time. The most successful organizations of the coming decades will be those led by frequency-intelligent leaders.

FQ Beside IQ and EQ

Alongside IQ (how we think) and EQ (how we relate), FQ measures how we align—our capacity to sustain coherent energy, act at the right time, and create without extraction.

This is why FQ belongs as a core dimension of human intelligence.

IQ measures cognitive ability—how well you process information, solve problems, and think analytically.

EQ measures emotional and relational skills—how well you understand feelings, navigate relationships, and influence others.

FQ measures resonance, how well you align with your natural rhythm, sustain yourself energetically, and create from coherence rather than force.

Where IQ helps us solve problems, and EQ helps us connect with others, FQ helps us sustain ourselves in a world of accelerating demands. Without it, even the most brilliant minds and the most emotionally intelligent leaders eventually collapse under the weight of misalignment.

The future belongs to those who can think clearly (IQ), relate skillfully (EQ), *AND* sustain themselves energetically (FQ). Organizations need people who can not only perform but also endure. Society needs leaders who can not only achieve but also model sustainability.

Consider what this looks like in practice:

High IQ, Low EQ, Low FQ. The brilliant individual who can solve complex problems but burns out their teams and themselves. They produce remarkable work in bursts but cannot sustain their output or their relationships.

High EQ, Low IQ, Low FQ. The emotionally intelligent person who understands people but cannot think strategically and exhausts themselves through overgiving. They create harmony but not progress.

High FQ, Low IQ, Low EQ. The aligned individual who sustains themselves well but cannot think complexly or relate effectively. They maintain their energy but are unable to impact others.

High IQ, High EQ, Low FQ. The brilliant, emotionally intelligent person who achieves remarkable things but eventually collapses. They can think and relate, but they cannot sustain.

The future requires all three intelligences working together. The capacity to think clearly, relate skillfully, and sustain energetically. This is the new definition of human intelligence—and the foundation of the new leadership we desperately need.

Without Frequency Intelligence, even the most gifted individuals eventually hit walls. They burn out despite their brilliance. They disconnect despite their emotional skills. They achieve success that they cannot maintain.

With Frequency Intelligence, people become unstoppable in a different way. Not because they can push through anything, but because they know how to align with everything. Not because they never encounter resistance, but because they know how to read resistance as guidance.

The Consciousness Evolution
Humanity's Next Intelligence

Just as emotional intelligence emerged in the 1990s and transformed our understanding of human capability, Frequency Intelligence represents the next stage in the evolution of consciousness. We are witnessing the birth of a new form of human awareness.

For centuries, humans have been unconsciously living inside their frequency patterns without recognizing them as intelligence. Now, for the first time, we can name, measure, and systematically develop this capacity. This isn't self-help—it's species development.

The people who develop Frequency Intelligence now will become the leaders, innovators, and creators who shape the future. Not because they survived the most dramatic breakdown, but because they learned to prevent breakdown altogether. They'll solve the sustainability crisis by first solving the human sustainability crisis.

This consciousness shift affects everything: how we raise children (honoring rhythm rather than forcing compliance), how we design organizations (stewardship rather than extraction), how we practice medicine (prevention through alignment rather than treatment after breakdown), how we define success (continuity over time rather than achievement through force).

We are at the beginning of recognizing humans as energetic beings with natural rhythms rather than machines that sometimes malfunction. This recognition will transform civilization.

Living the Shift

What does daily life look like when someone begins thinking in frequency terms rather than diagnostic categories? The changes are both subtle and profound.

Morning Rhythms. Instead of forcing the same routine regardless of energy state, you begin each day by checking in with your system. What phase are you in? What does your energy feel like? A Launch morning gets ambitious projects. A Reflect morning benefits from quiet planning or restoration. You stop fighting your natural rhythm and start surfing it.

Decision-Making Through Frequency. When opportunities arise, instead of asking "Should I do this?" you ask "Does this align with my current frequency?" You feel into your body's response—expansion or contraction, ease or resistance. You schedule important decisions during Peak windows rather than when you feel depleted.

Boundary Setting with Precision. Instead of feeling guilty about saying no, you develop precise language:

I'm at capacity this week; I can revisit next Tuesday.	I can do A or B, not both. Which is higher leverage?
I'm in a Reflect phase; let's schedule a deep conversation after the 15th.	This needs my Peak window. I'll send it by 11 a.m. tomorrow.

Your boundaries become information, not rejection.

Seasonal Life Planning. You start designing your year around natural energy cycles rather than arbitrary calendar dates—quarter themes based on your frequency needs. Bold moves are scheduled during Launch seasons. Reflection time is incorporated into the calendar before you need it, not after you collapse.

Workflow Redesign. You match tasks to energy states: creative work during Peak windows, administrative tasks during Low periods. You protect your most valuable cognitive hours instead of squandering them on email. You batch similar activities and create transition rituals between different types of work.

The shift isn't dramatic—it's intelligent. You stop pushing through resistance and start reading it as guidance. You stop managing symptoms and start preventing misalignment. You stop surviving your life and start designing it.

The Frequency-Literate Future

Imagine a world where Frequency Intelligence is as fundamental as reading and writing. Where children learn to recognize their energy patterns alongside their ABCs. Where this isn't revolutionary—it's simply how conscious humans organize their lives.

Education Redesigned. Schools are configured around natural learning rhythms rather than administrative convenience. Movement is integrated throughout the day. Quiet spaces are available for introverted students. High-stimulation environments exist for those who thrive on intensity. Assessment methods recognize and value different forms of intelligence and developmental timing.

Healthcare Evolution. Medical appointments include an energetic assessment alongside a physical examination. Doctors are trained to recognize when symptoms might be frequency misalignment rather than pathology. Preventive care focuses on sustainable living patterns, not just disease management.

Workplace Transformation. Organizations are created as living ecosystems rather than mechanical systems. Leadership development focuses on frequency stewardship. Performance metrics include sustainability and congruity, not just output. Work environments support rather than fight human neurology.

Urban Planning with Frequency in Mind. Cities are configured for human rhythms—quiet zones, natural light, green spaces for restoration. Public spaces accommodate different energy needs and sensory preferences. Transportation systems honor natural timing rather than forcing uniform schedules.

Technology Aligned with Biology. Digital tools are engineered to support rather than fragment attention. Apps remind us to honor our rhythms rather than override them. Technology enhances human frequency rather than disrupting it.

This future isn't a utopian fantasy. It's practical evolution—the next step in human development as we learn to work with our nature rather than against it.

The Cultural Tipping Point
When Breakdown Culture Becomes Primitive

We are approaching a moment when diagnosis culture will seem as primitive as bloodletting. When performing trauma for recognition will feel as outdated as hiding mental health struggles. When forcing humans into machine rhythms will appear as barbaric as child labor.

This tipping point happens when enough individuals model a different way:

Leaders demonstrate sustainable success. Parents raise children who trust their signals.

Educators honor natural development.

Healthcare providers support alignment alongside treatment.

The transformation won't be dramatic or sudden. It will be quiet, irreversible, and person by person. Each individual who chooses frequency over pathology, alignment over attachment, and presence over performance creates permission for others to do the same.

We are witnessing the birth of a new culture— one organized around human thriving rather than human surviving, around preventing collapse rather than monetizing it, around sustainable power rather than dramatic breakdown.
This is not a revolution—it's a return to coherence.

We are remembering the frequency intelligence that exists in our deepest biology—the same organizing wisdom that governs natural cycles, cellular rhythms, and how life itself maintains sustainable flow.

The future belongs to those who recognize that their frequency is their guidance, their rhythm is their resource, and their alignment is their authority.

This is not just personal development. This is species evolution, and it begins with understanding that you are not broken—you are broadcasting. The world is finally ready to listen.

The Unfashionable Promise

If you've ever felt like you had to prove your value through pain—I want you to know: You don't.

If you've ever wondered whether your struggles make you broken—they don't. They make you human.

If you've ever felt guilty for not keeping up with a pace that feels inhuman—the pace is the problem, not you.

Your frequency is enough. Your timing is valid. You don't have to be bleeding to be powerful. You don't have to collapse to be seen. You're not late. You're not broken. You're not behind.

You are broadcasting—now learning to tune.

This is the invitation of Frequency Intelligence: to step out of the performance of pain and into the power of alignment. To trade diagnosis for discernment. To choose rhythm over resistance.

The future belongs to those who learn to read their signals, honor their rhythm, and build their lives from alignment rather than force.

This book doesn't offer spectacle; it offers a practice. Test with care, lead with humility, design with precision. Stop rewarding collapse. Build emotional infrastructure that lasts.

Frequency Intelligence is culturally new, yes. That's why it matters. We did not know. Now we can learn.

You're not late. You're not behind. You're right on time to begin. You are not broken. You are signaling.

From Calibration to Stewardship

You're not malfunctioning—you're signalling. FQ doesn't replace medicine or therapy; it restores timing and agency so fewer people reach collapse in the first place. But this can't stop at personal practice. The next chapter asks a larger question: how do we remain sovereign as intelligent tools accelerate around us? Astrology as a compass, wearables as mirrors, algorithms as dashboards—useful, not decisive. The leadership of life is still human. Chapter 8 is the covenant with that leadership.

PRACTICAL APPLICATIONS
FREQUENCY TOOLKIT

The following section provides concrete tools and protocols for implementing Frequency Intelligence in daily life and organizations.

A Seven-Day Frequency Audit

Day 1—Track Inputs

List all inputs (notifications, conversations, spaces, foods, tasks). Note which adds clarity and which adds noise.

Day 2—Map Peaks

Notice 90-minute windows where thinking is clean. Repeat patterns across days—those are your Peak blocks.

Day 3—Notice Nerves

Track micro-signals: jaw clench, chest tightness, shallow breath, eye strain. These are early-warning data points.

Day 4—Environment Scan

Which spaces energize? Which drain? (light, noise, air, visual clutter)

Day 5—People Patterns

After time with X, do you feel resourced or depleted? Frequency is relational.

Day 6—Task Fit

Pair tasks to energy: ideation in Peak, admin in Low.

Day 7—Synthesis

Draft your first Frequency Charter:

My Peak windows:_____

My Low windows:_____

Inputs I'm limiting:_____

Spaces I'm choosing for deep work:_____

Weekly Reflect time:_____

Update monthly.

The Daily Alignment Check-In (Three Minutes)

- **Body:** What's tight? What's warm?
- **Breath:** Take an extended exhale for sixty seconds.
- **Timing:** Which phase am I in (Reflect/Gather/Launch/Sustain)?
- **Move:** What is the cleanest next step given that phase?
- **Boundary:** What gets a "no" today to protect this step?

Reflect (inward, integrating): protect quiet, fewer inputs, long-form reading, walks without audio

Gather (curious, resourcing): research, interviews, refining questions, slow meetings with whiteboards

Launch (decisive, outward): ship drafts, present, make calls, commit

Sustain (maintain, refine): process feedback, systematize, support

Misery happens when you Launch in Reflect or Sustain in empty tanks.

Language Translation Guide

Replace diagnostic language with frequency precision:

- I'm anxious. → My inputs are too high for my processing pace.

- I'm burned out. → I've been in output without restoration.

- I'm procrastinating. → My energy is resisting forced motion; I need a timing change.

- I'm lazy. → I'm in Reflect; production returns after integration.

- I can't focus. → My environment and task don't match.

The Five-Signal Decision Filter

Before saying yes, check:

Body: Constriction or ease?

Timing: Does this land in a Launch window?

Values: Does this serve the longer arc?

Capacity: What gets dropped to make room?

Recovery: Where's the restoration that follows?

If three or more signals flash red, the answer is no—or not now.

Seasonal Planning—Quarterly

Quarter Theme: One guiding frequency (e.g., Build, Prune, Seed, Stabilize)	**Two Non-Negotiables:** Health and one relationship practice
One Bold Move: A Launch aligned with the theme	**Reflect Weeks:** Put them on the calendar first

Organizational Design Principles
For leaders ready to implement Frequency Intelligence at scale:

Rhythmic Calendaring: Replace uniform eight-hour days with energy-aware blocks of time. Team members declare Peak, Steady, and Low windows.

Meeting Hygiene: Half the meetings, half the length. No meeting is held inside anyone's declared Peak block unless it is deemed mission-critical.

Autonomy Windows: Guarantee at least one protected two-hour block daily for uninterrupted deep work.

Environment by Function: Quiet zones for focus; collaborative zones for interaction; transition zones for decompression.

Energy Budgets: Treat attention like a finite asset. Projects receive an energy budget in addition to cost/time.

Seasonal Sprints: Plan launches in natural waves. Insert formal Reflect weeks between sprints.

Five Tiny Practices That Cost Nothing

1. Close three tabs before opening a new one.

2. Stand to transition between phases (thirty seconds).

3. Write the next micro-step at the end of each session.

4. Name the phase out loud before you start.

5. Protect the first ten minutes of your Peak window, meaning no checking of your inbox.

Personal and Leader Vows

A Personal Vow—Use or Adapt

- I will listen for warmth and tightness before I listen for timelines.

- I will schedule my peaks, protect my Reflect, and declare my no.

- I will not perform my pain for permission.

- I will let seasons season me.

- I will remember: I am not broken. I am broadcasting

A Leader's Vow—Use or Adapt

- I will not win by burning through people.

- I will design for peaks and protection.

- I will publish my own rhythms, invite others to do the same, and respect the differences that exist among us.

- I will measure outcomes that structural rhythm makes possible—quality, retention, learning—alongside speed.

- I will fix systems before I fix people.

One-Liners to Anchor the Approach

- Sustainability is not a corporate value; it's a human metabolism.

- Labels can legitimize pain; rhythm can liberate it.

- You don't need a new personality; you need a new tempo.

- Urgency is a liar when timing is unclear.

- Coherence is contagious.

CHAPTER 8

The Human Frequency
The Beginning of an Ending

This is not a finale. It's ignition.

When I look at the world right now, I don't just see change. I see collapse and creation happening simultaneously. Old Systems are crumbling. Economies, politics, leadership models, and new ones are emerging, often quietly, at the edges.

The question I keep returning to is this: Will we evolve consciously or unconsciously?

That's why I wrote this book. That's why Frequency Intelligence exists.

Not as another framework to manage your calendar, or another productivity tool to squeeze more out of already exhausted humans, but as a living system to remind us of what we've forgotten:

We are rhythmic beings.	Timing matters more than force.
Frequency is intelligence.	The future will not be led by who controls the most data, but by who lives the most aligned.

We are entering an age where technology will outthink us, outcalculate us, and outpredict us, but technology cannot out-feel us. It cannot embody, intuit, or integrate. That is our domain, and if we don't strengthen that domain and reclaim it, then yes, machines will take over. Not because they are evil, but because we forgot who we are.

This chapter is not just a conclusion. It's a compass. A manifesto. A mirror for the future we are already building, whether consciously or not.

From People to Products Back to People
The Full Circle

When I look back at my own path, I see a circle.

I began with people. I studied culture, communication, and identity. I was fascinated by the invisible forces that shape us. I worked with leaders and organizations, helping them make sense of values, sustainability, and meaning. My focus was human—always human.

Then I shifted to product. I poured years of my life into ReyRey, believing that if I could just make fashion more sustainable—if I could design shoes that lasted—I could help the planet heal. It was sincere. It was beautiful. It was needed. Still, it was also incomplete.

Because you can design all the sustainable products in the world, but if the humans—making them, selling them, wearing them—are burned out, disconnected, and misaligned, nothing truly changes. Now, almost without planning it, I have come back to people. To human sustainability. To the realization that the most unsustainable thing in our world right now is not plastic, not carbon, not even politics. It is the human nervous system running beyond its natural limits.

That is the full circle. From people, to products, back to people again. From culture to fashion, back to frequency.

The new sustainability isn't just environmental. It's energetic. Emotional. Human.

Learning to Reset
From Ashram to Inner Architecture

The first time I needed a reset was more than ten years ago. My life at that time had come to an end. The life I had built felt like rubble, and I didn't know how to begin again. So I left. I went to India. I spent a month in an ashram and two months traveling, and for the first three weeks, I did nothing but cry. I cried for the life I had lost, for the weight of expectations I could no longer carry, for the emptiness I felt inside.

Yet, that season of grief became the soil for something new. By removing myself from everything familiar, I learned that collapse could also be a portal. I began to rebuild, not through force, but through listening. That trip was my first reset. The moment I realized that sometimes you need to step outside your life to find ... something I didn't have words for yet.

In the ashram, stripped of my roles and routines, I discovered something I had never noticed in my busy life: I had an inner rhythm. Not just a schedule or a productivity cycle, but something more enthralling that pulsed beneath all my doing. When I stopped forcing outcomes and started paying attention to when I felt expansive, when I needed to withdraw, and when clarity emerged, I began to understand the foundation of everything I now know about alignment and timing.

Now, a decade later, I find myself in another reset. But this time, I didn't have to leave for an ashram. This time, I've learned to create the space within myself. The same silence. The same release. The same rebuilding. What once required leaving everything behind now happens from the inside out.

What once required a monastery of walls now lives as architecture within me.

This is what Frequency Intelligence makes possible: carrying your reset with you, wherever you are. External tools, such as astrology, AI, and biofeedback, can support this inner architecture. However, they can never replace the fundamental human capacity to sense when you're aligned and when you need to recalibrate.

That decade between resets taught me the difference between breakdown and breakthrough. Breakdown happens when we ignore our frequencies until the system forces a crisis. Breakthrough happens when we learn to read the early frequencies and respond before collapse becomes necessary.

The frequency was always there. I just hadn't learned to trust it yet.

I Wish Someone Had Told Me

I sometimes wish someone had helped me live and work in alignment earlier.

Instead, I did what everyone does. I followed the invisible frameworks: work hard, achieve success, earn money, buy things, and feel accomplished only through the outer metrics.

And yes, I succeeded. I ticked the boxes, but the feeling was hollow. I was mentally drained, restless, and misaligned, yet I felt filled with energy. I knew something was wrong, but I didn't have the words for it.

Looking back, I can see what was actually happening: my system was sending me information. Though without the language of frequency literacy, I interpreted these signals as personal failings. Without a framework for alignment, I assumed chronic exhaustion was simply the cost of success.

The chronic fatigue I experienced in my thirties wasn't a medical mystery. It was my system saying this path is unsustainable." The dissatisfaction that would spike during certain business meetings wasn't a character flaw. It was intelligence telling me *this partnership is misaligned.* The restlessness that would overtake me after achieving goals wasn't ingratitude. It was my frequency whispering, *This isn't your authentic path.*

238

In retrospect, I had been trained, like most of us, to override these frequencies. To push through discomfort. To solve problems with willpower, rationale, and data rather than wisdom. To treat my body like a machine that should operate the same way regardless of cycles, seasons, or inner weather patterns.

That's what I want future humans to know: success that comes at the cost of your coherence is not true success. It's just a prettier form of collapse.

Your restlessness isn't rebellion. It's intelligence.

Your sensitivity isn't weakness. It's precision.

Your need for rhythm isn't limitation. It's optimization.

Frequency Speaks Before the Mind Interprets

Here's what I've learned: frequency is always broadcasting. Always. The question is whether we've developed the literacy to decode what it's telling us.

When I say "frequency," I mean the felt broadcast of your inner timing and alignment—translated into something usable.

Your frequency communicates through energy shifts, physical sensations, emotional responses, timing impulses, and even through what you resist or what repeatedly captures your attention. It doesn't speak in words. It speaks in the language of the nervous system.

Sadly, our culture has systematically trained us to trust external authority over our own internal knowing. We follow GPS into lakes (I did that myself). We let recommendation algorithms decide what we watch, read, and think. We measure our worth by metrics that have nothing to do with our actual contribution to life.

When we mistake external guidance for our internal frequency, we hand over our sovereignty.

This is why tools become essential—not because they ARE the intelligence, but because they give us language for the unlanguageable.

Astrology becomes our compass—not because the stars control us, but because planetary movements give us vocabulary for energetic weather patterns we can feel but can't name. When I say "Mercury is retrograde," I'm not suggesting the planet is causing communication breakdowns. I'm acknowledging that there are cycles when reflection serves better than initiation, when slowing down reveals more than speeding up.

AI becomes our mirror, not because algorithms understand consciousness, but because pattern recognition helps us see our own patterns more clearly. Machine learning can identify correlations between my energy levels and external factors that I might overlook in the complexity of daily life. But the interpretation, the meaning-making, that's still mine.

Biometric tracking becomes translation, not because devices know our truth, but because data can help us see what our bodies are already broadcasting. Heart Rate Variability doesn't tell me how to live, but it can reveal the physiological impact of different choices, different environments, and different relationships.

The tools are training wheels for trusting what you already know.

Remember: the intelligence is you; the rest is translation.

The Three Pillars of Sovereign Intelligence

Think of your future capacity as a tripod. Remove any leg, and the structure collapses.

- Skill in analysis, strategy, and discernment.

- Essential, but insufficient alone.

- A crystal mind can cut the wrong thing.

- I've seen brilliant people make terrible decisions because they could analyze data but couldn't read timing.

- They understood the logic but missed the frequency.

EQ (Emotional/Relational Intelligence): Coherence

- Capacity to feel, relate, and influence without manipulation.

- Crucial, but can become performative if ungrounded.

- Emotional intelligence without energetic intelligence often leads to people-pleasing, burnout from over-giving, or manipulation disguised as empathy.

FQ (Frequency Intelligence): Calibration

- Ability to read energetic states, align actions to timing, and regulate your nervous system in real time.

- This is the missing piece that makes IQ precise and EQ authentic.

- With FQ, you know not just what to do and how to do it relationally, but when to do it and whether it's truly yours to do.

- With FQ, your IQ becomes right-sized and your EQ becomes right-timed.

- You stop solving the wrong problems beautifully and start solving the right problems precisely.

This is not about competing with machines. It's about becoming more human than ever. It's about strengthening our inner frequency so we don't hand over our sovereignty to technology.

FQ Non-Negotiables

- Tools inform; humans decide.

- Timing outranks pressure.

- Coherence precedes scale.

> The frequency is what machines can never simulate. The frequency is our guarantee of remaining authors rather than artifacts.

Machines Can Compute Humans Must Choose

A car is faster than a human.

A plane crosses continents we could never walk.

But we never said, "The airplane is now in charge of humanity."

We built it, we steer it, we land it.

The same must be true for the technologies of this century. We can coexist with intelligent systems without outsourcing our sovereignty. We can design systems that amplify wisdom, not replace it. We can choose presence over automation.

Yes, machines will surpass us in processing power, knowledge storage, and prediction. In many ways, they already have. The machines will be smarter, faster, and "wiser" in the ways of logic than we could ever be.

Keep in mind that wisdom is not the same as intelligence, intelligence is not the same as consciousness, and consciousness is not the same as frequency.

The real question is not whether machines will outthink us. It's whether we will let them out-choose us.

The frequency contains qualities that no model can ever simulate: embodied timing that reads the energetic field of a moment, ethical imagination that considers consequences across generations, meaning-making rooted in lived experience and personal values, and the uniquely human alchemy of courage under genuine uncertainty.

That's the difference between computation and consciousness. Machines can calculate the most effective communication strategy, but they cannot carry the genuine presence, care, and accountability that only humans can embody.

The frequency is what makes the difference. The frequency is what people sense. The frequency cannot be faked or outsourced.

The moment we hand over the decision-making to the tool, we become passengers in our own lives. The frequency becomes static.

War as Old-School Leadership

Wars are not only fought with guns and tanks. They are fought in workplaces, in families, in marriages, in markets. Wars are the language of force, the childish ultimatum: Do as I say, or else.

War is what happens when leadership is based on force instead of frequency. It's the child saying, "Do as I say or I'll hit you." It's the boss saying, "Do it my way or you're fired." It's the government saying, "Obey or we'll punish you."

It's primitive. It's reactive. It's unsustainable.

Yet, many still believe that it is power. They believe domination equals leadership. What they don't see is that this very model is crumbling beneath their feet because, although force may win in the short term, frequency always wins in the long term.

Sometimes I still cannot comprehend how little we have learned from history. In our current lifetime, we live in a world with more active wars than ever before. Leaders and politicians still cling to the same outdated playbooks of force and fear. Entire nations act like children in a playground, screaming, threatening, and hitting.

I ask myself: Where are people's minds? Where is self-thinking? Where are values, presence, sovereignty?

We have more access to information than any civilization in history, yet we continue to repeat the same patterns. We can communicate instantly across continents, yet we struggle to communicate effectively across a negotiation table. We have technologies that could solve most of humanity's practical problems, yet we use them to amplify our oldest conflicts.

This is what happens when we advance our outer technologies without evolving our inner architecture. We create more sophisticated ways to wage the same primitive wars. We build smarter weapons to fight stupider conflicts. We use 21st-century tools to express Stone Age emotions.

Then I look closer, and I see: it begins small. If you fight with your neighbor about a fence or a plant, if you cannot hold dialogue about land, about boundaries, about respect, why would nations be any different? Consider unregulated energy scales: a garden dispute escalates into a border war.

Every empire instituted on fear eventually falls. Every leader who ruled by intimidation eventually lost their throne. Every family held together by control eventually fractured.

Why? Because alignment is stronger than aggression. Frequency is stronger than noise. Coherence is stronger than coercion.

Frequency-based leadership replaces war with coherence. It replaces "Do as I say" with "Let's find the frequency we share." It replaces force with flow, ultimatums with alignment, and fear with timing.

In my consulting work, I've seen the transformation happen repeatedly. Organizations in crisis often act when their force-based leadership has led to high turnover, low morale, and innovation stagnation. The presenting problems vary, but the root cause is usually the same: leadership operating from a state of override rather than one of frequency awareness.

The shift from force to frequency isn't soft or weak. It's precise. It means reading the energetic state of a team before making demands. It means having difficult conversations at a time when people can actually hear them. It means building sustainable motivation rather than manufacturing artificial urgency. It means choosing influence over intimidation, every single time.

The real enemy isn't another nation, another company, another person. The real enemy is misalignment—operating disconnected from our authentic frequency.

When we operate from frequency alignment, we don't need to fight. We collaborate. We innovate. We create solutions that serve everyone involved. When we operate from frequency override, we generate conflict, resistance, and eventually, some form of warfare.

This is why frequency-based leadership isn't just more effective. It's the only sustainable way forward.

Generational Responsibility Building Humans Who Last

When I think about the future, I don't just think about myself or even my children. I think about the generations that will come after them. Gen Alpha. Gen Beta. Whatever names come next. Future humans who will inherit the systems we are creating right now.

Here is where I feel the deepest responsibility:

We are raising the first generation of humans who will have access to more information than any generation in history, yet potentially less capacity to discern what that information actually means for their lives.

This isn't about technology being bad. This is about a fundamental shift in how humans develop their decision-making capabilities.

Let me trace the frequency through the generations:

Baby Boomers sculpted structures of order and industry. They created systems, accumulated wealth, and established institutions. Their gift was expansion and ambition. Their shadow was often overriding natural limits, both environmental and human, in the service of growth. Their frequency: "Build and accumulate."

Gen X learned to adapt in the cracks between collapsing ideals and emerging realities. They became fiercely independent, skeptical of systems, resourceful in chaos. Their gift was resilience through scarcity. Their shadow was often cynicism and disconnection from collective purpose. Their frequency: "Survive and adapt."

Millennials inherited the contradictions, were raised to follow rules that collapsed beneath them, and were blamed for economic crises they didn't create. They became the first generation to name burnout as a systemic problem rather than personal failure. Their gift was challenging unsustainable systems. Their shadow was often paralysis from overwhelm and perfectionism. Their frequency: "Question and optimize."

Gen Zers are digital natives, brilliant, creative, globally aware, and socially conscious. They can navigate complexity that would have overwhelmed previous generations. Their gift is fluid intelligence and the ability to rapidly adapt. Their shadow is often fragility under pressure and addiction to external validation through digital feedback loops. Their frequency: "Feel and express."

Gen Alpha is growing up in a world where AI is not new. It's normal. They will never know a time before intelligent machines. Their challenge will not be access to information, but access to their own inner knowing. Their gift could be seamless human-AI collaboration. Their shadow could be complete dependence on external intelligence. Their frequency: "Integrate and discern."

Then comes the generation we haven't named yet: the children of Alpha, the ones who will inherit a fully AI-integrated world. They may never experience the friction between human and artificial intelligence that we're navigating now. For them, the distinction might be as natural as the difference between thinking and speaking. But will they know their own frequency? Will they maintain human agency in a world of infinite artificial capability? Their frequency: "Still forming."

What Today's Leaders Must Do Differently

If you are a parent, teacher, manager, or leader of any kind, you carry unprecedented responsibility. You are literally shaping the humans who will determine whether our species remains sovereign in an AI-integrated future.

For Parents:
Stop teaching compliance. Start teaching frequency literacy. When your child says they're tired, hungry, or overwhelmed, honor that information instead of overriding it for convenience. Teach them that their body broadcasts valuable data, not obstacles to efficiency.

Create rhythm-aware households. Notice when your child naturally focuses best, needs social connection, or requires quiet time. Design family life around these patterns rather than forcing everyone into the same schedule.

Model emotional regulation instead of demanding it. Show them how you read your own frequencies, how you respond to stress, and how you make decisions based on alignment rather than reaction. Children learn more from what they observe than what they're told.

For Educators:
Design educational environments that honor individual learning styles and frequencies. Some students focus better in motion, while others concentrate better in stillness. Some people learn best in the morning, while others learn best in the afternoon. Stop treating these differences as problems to be corrected.

Teach nervous system literacy alongside academic subjects. Help students recognize when they're overstimulated, understimulated, or optimally regulated. These skills will serve them more than most of what they memorize.

Replace standardized testing with authentic assessment during optimal timing windows for each student. Measure frequency strength, not just information retention.

For Organizational Leaders:
Stop measuring face time and start measuring frequency contour. Is your team operating from sustainable energy or artificial stimulation? Are people contributing from their zone of strength or grinding through misalignment?

Design work around human frequency patterns rather than industrial convenience. Not everyone's deep work happens from nine to five. Not everyone's creativity flows during scheduled brainstorming sessions.

Train managers in frequency literacy. Teach them to recognize when someone is operating from burnout, when the timing is optimal for difficult conversations, and when a project is being forced rather than flowing.

The Collective Challenge:
We must raise humans who can maintain their frequency integrity while collaborating effectively with artificial intelligence. This means building strong internal guidance systems before handing them external tools.

Previous generations had to develop internal navigation systems because external guidance wasn't readily available. They learned to read social cues because they couldn't text instead of having difficult conversations. They developed tolerance for frustration because instant gratification wasn't an option. They built attention muscles because distraction wasn't engineered to be more engaging than reality.

We've inadvertently created an environment that doesn't require these capabilities to develop.

Every child is born with natural frequency literacy. They know when they're tired, when they need connection, when something feels right or wrong. If we consistently override these frequencies for convenience—teaching them to trust external systems more than internal knowing—we're preparing them for a future where they'll be perfectly suited to be guided by artificial intelligence rather than their own intelligence.

The stakes are generational sovereignty.

The children raised today will either become the most discerning, resilient, and frequency-literate generation in history, or they will become the first generation to live primarily as passengers in algorithmically guided lives.

Every generation believes it is preparing the succeeding one for future success. Most often, we are actually preparing them for a world that no longer exists.

We train children to memorize information while search engines provide instant access to humanity's accumulated knowledge. We insist they sit motionless and follow predetermined instructions when their future will demand cognitive flexibility and creative problem-solving. We reward obedience and rule-compliance when their era will require sovereignty and independent critical thinking.

Generation Z already demonstrates the fracture lines. They possess remarkable capabilities, including digital fluency, a global perspective, social consciousness, and creative innovation. Yet, they also exhibit concerning vulnerabilities: chronic overstimulation, anxiety disorders, attention regulation difficulties, and validation dependency on external systems.

If we do not fundamentally transform how we guide emerging generations, they will surrender their power to machines, not out of laziness but from learned helplessness. They will choose algorithmic decision-making because no institution taught them to trust and develop their own inner guidance systems.

Future humans will not survive—let alone thrive—if educated only to memorize, perform, and comply with external systems. They will require inner strength that matches outer acceleration. Psychological resistance to manipulation. Capacity to hold paradox without paralysis. Skills to navigate both digital and energetic domains with genuine sovereignty.

Frequency Intelligence matters because it represents not just personal alignment technology. It is generational sustainability infrastructure. Current movements focus on sustainable products, business models, and environmental practices. Now we must focus on sustainable humans. Human beings who do not burn out by thirty, disconnect by forty, or become obsolete by fifty because they never learned authentic self-leadership.

The incorrect question: *Will AI outsmart humans?*

The essential question: *Will humans remain strong enough to lead themselves?*

The difference will come down to whether we teach them to strengthen their inner frequency or to bypass it for external convenience.

A New Kind of Sustainability

We often talk about sustainability in the context of products, climate, or energy. But what about sustainable humans? What about building inner systems that can withstand the speed, complexity, and chaos of the world that is coming?

The sustainability movement focused on what we consumed, how we produced, and where we sourced materials. The next evolution must focus on how we sustain the humans doing the consuming, producing, and sourcing. It must address the epidemic of burnout, anxiety, and disconnection that makes even the most environmentally conscious ventures feel hollow.

Consider the irony: we design products to last decades while designing work lives that burn out humans in months. We optimize supply chains for efficiency while creating management chains that drain human energy. We measure carbon footprints while ignoring the energetic footprints of our organizational designs.

We create algorithms that learn and adapt, while building educational systems that demand conformity and suppress natural learning rhythms. We develop artificial intelligence that processes information at superhuman speeds, while maintaining human institutions that operate at industrial-age pace.

We engineer devices with sophisticated user interfaces that respond to our slightest touch, while designing human interfaces, such as meetings, performance reviews, and organizational communication, that feel clunky and unresponsive to actual human needs.

The disconnect is staggering. We apply more design thinking to a smartphone screen than to the daily experience of the humans using it. We invest more in optimizing website user experience than in optimizing human work experience. We spend more time debugging software than debugging the human systems that create the software.

This isn't just about individual well-being. It's about systemic sustainability. Unsustainable humans create unsustainable systems. Depleted leaders make depleted decisions. Exhausted teams produce exhausted innovations. Burned-out parents raise anxious children who become overwhelmed adults who perpetuate the cycle.

The symptoms are everywhere: rising rates of anxiety and depression, widespread burnout across all sectors, political polarization that mirrors nervous system dysregulation, environmental destruction that reflects our disconnection from natural rhythms, and technological addiction that substitutes artificial stimulation for authentic satisfaction. I don't even need to pull out the numbers and research because we know this, yet we still struggle to change.

These aren't separate problems requiring separate solutions. They're manifestations of the same root cause: humans operating chronically disconnected from their own frequency.

This is why I say that sustainability is not only about products; it's about people. True sustainability must be energetic. Emotional. Human. We need humans who are themselves durable, capable of thriving across decades rather than sprinting through quarters.

Resilience as Curriculum

Resilience is not a personality trait. It's a curriculum.

It is assembled through micro-choices: holding discomfort without collapse, delaying gratification, practicing boundaries, and building coherence. It's teaching children and adults alike to strengthen their nervous systems instead of outsourcing their regulation to screens, substances, or algorithms.

The kind of resilience that today's and future generations need is different from what previous generations required. Previous generations built resilience through scarcity, through survival, through physical challenges. Today's generations must build resilience through abundance, encompassing a wealth of choices, information, stimulation, and possibilities.

Traditional resilience training taught you to endure hardship.

Modern resilience training teaches you to navigate complexity without losing your frequency.

Morning Frequency Check (three minutes)
Before consuming any external information, such as news, emails, or social media, take three minutes to scan your internal landscape. What's your energy level? What's your emotional state? What does your body need? What's your capacity for the day? This isn't self-indulgence; it's Frequency Intelligence.

Decision-Point Pauses (thirty seconds)
Before making any decision about what to eat, how to respond to a message, or whether to take on a new commitment, pause and check your frequency. Does this choice feel expansive or contractive in your body? Are you choosing from alignment or reaction? Are you operating from your authentic timing or artificial urgency?

Evening Frequency Review (five minutes)
End each day by reviewing: When did you honor your frequency today? When did you override it? What were the consequences of each choice? What patterns do you notice? This builds frequency literacy through conscious reflection.

Monthly and Seasonal Frequency Calibration

Signal Audit
Once monthly, assess: Are you living according to your authentic frequency or someone else's expectations? What adjustments need to be made? What patterns need to be interrupted? What support do you need?

Timing Review
Look back at major decisions from the past month. Which ones did you make during aligned timing? Which were forced? What can you learn about your optimal decision-making windows?

Frequency Strengthening

Each month, add one practice that strengthens your frequency literacy. Cold exposure that teaches nervous system regulation. Meditation that builds attention control. Fasting that clarifies the difference between authentic need and habitual reaction.

Seasonal Recalibration

Every three months, conduct an intensive frequency review. How has your natural rhythm evolved? What external factors are supporting or disrupting your frequency? What needs to shift in your environment, relationships, or commitments to maintain coherence?

Annual Frequency Architecture

Once a year, design your life around your deepest, most resonant frequency patterns. What are your optimal work rhythms? Your natural relationship cycles? Your authentic creative seasons? Build your calendar, your commitments, and your goals around these patterns rather than fighting them.

Cultural Signal Practices

Frequency Cleansing

Spend at least one hour per week in complete digital silence. No devices, no inputs, no distractions. Just you and your unmediated frequency. Notice what emerges when the noise stops.

Boundary Practice

Each week, practice saying no to one thing that doesn't align with your frequency, even if it's convenient or expected. Practice saying yes to one thing that does align, even if it feels uncomfortable or uncertain.

When your nervous system becomes overloaded, have a specific sequence in mind for returning to baseline. This might include breathing techniques, movement, time in nature, or specific sensory inputs that help you recalibrate. Build the capacity to feel anxiety without being controlled by it, to sit with uncertainty without rushing to premature solutions, to experience disappointment without interpreting it as evidence of personal inadequacy.

Advanced frequency training involves learning to distinguish between different types of internal frequencies, such as fear-based resistance versus intuitive guidance, authentic tiredness versus avoidance, and healthy boundaries versus isolation. This precision prevents misinterpreting important information and supports the development of the capacity to read not just your own frequency but the energetic state of groups, teams, and communities.

If we want future humans to survive, not just technically, but spiritually, we must build resilience as a practice. Sensitivity without skill becomes overwhelm. Sensitivity with skill becomes precision and power.

This is the work of generational responsibility: not to leave them more stuff, but to leave them more frequency strength.

Why Old Maps Can't Guide Us

The systems we inherited were cultivated for a different age. Schools are scripted for another type of life. Corporations are modeled after militaries. Leadership is rooted in hierarchy and control.

However, we are no longer living in the 1950s. We are living in a world of constant acceleration. AI is training faster than laws, children are absorbing more information in a day than our grandparents did in a year, and ecosystems and economies are collapsing under the weight of extraction.

The frameworks that got us here cannot take us where we need to go.

Consider education: We still organize schools around industrial schedules, starting at the same time, moving through subjects in predetermined sequences, and measuring success through standardized testing. Yet we now know that humans have individual chronotypes, that different types of learning require different energetic states, and that creativity and analytical thinking operate on different frequencies.

Consider healthcare: We still treat symptoms rather than addressing the energetic and lifestyle factors that create disease. We medicate anxiety and depression without teaching nervous system regulation. We manage chronic conditions without exploring the relationship between frequency override and physical breakdown.

Consider leadership: We still promote people based on technical competence or political maneuvering rather than their capacity to steward energy, read timing, or create sustainable team dynamics. We reward overwork and undervalue restoration. We measure productivity but ignore frequency coherence.

Yet, we continue trying to solve modern complexity with outdated theories. Old management systems. Old motivational models. Old leadership archetypes.

This is why workplaces feel like battlefields, why families feel like fractured teams, and why politics looks like war in suits.

We are still applying old maps to new terrain.

The map suggests that success requires the sacrifice of well-being. The map that says leadership means control rather than frequency coherence. The map that says productivity matters more than sustainability. The map that says external metrics determine internal worth.

These maps might have served in simpler times, but they create chaos in our current complexity.

Frequency Intelligence does not discard the past. It simply says *the past is not enough.* We need updated maps for our current terrain. Maps that account for the speed of change, the volume of information, the pressure of global interconnectedness, and the reality of human nervous systems that evolved for much simpler circumstances.

Frequency-based maps for a frequency-rich world.

A Future Worth Building

I don't want to end this book with a critique alone. I want to conclude with a vision.

What would it look like if frequency became the cultural foundation, not the exception?

Education Redesigned Around Human Frequency

Imagine schools where children begin each day with a three-minute frequency check: "Where am I today? Launch, Align, or Reflect?" Teachers understand that attention spans vary not just by age but by individual chronotype, seasonal cycles, and collective energy patterns.

Learning environments include quiet spaces for individuals with overstimulated nervous systems and movement areas for kinesthetic processors. Classrooms have adjustable lighting that responds to natural circadian rhythms and individual sensory needs. Sound design considers acoustic sensitivity rather than assuming all students can focus in the same auditory environment.

The curriculum is delivered through multiple modalities simultaneously—visual, auditory, kinesthetic, energetic—so students can engage through their strongest frequency pathways. Assessment occurs during optimal timing windows for each child rather than arbitrary testing schedules that favor some learning styles over others.

Teachers receive training in nervous system development, trauma-informed education, and individual frequency recognition. They learn to distinguish between behavioral problems and frequency mismatches: the child who needs movement to focus, the one who requires extra processing time, and the one who learns best in collaborative environments.

Students graduate fluent not only in academic subjects but in frequency literacy, nervous system regulation, and collaborative timing. They understand their personal rhythms as clearly as they know mathematical principles. They can read their own frequencies as naturally as they read text.

Most importantly, they maintain their capacity for independent thought while collaborating effectively with AI systems. They know the difference between information and wisdom, between data and frequency, between artificial intelligence and authentic knowing.

Workplaces Aligned with Human Architecture

Envision organizations where schedules reflect individual deep-work chronotypes rather than industrial conveniences. Meetings happen during collective energy peaks, not default time slots. Project deadlines account for natural work rhythms rather than artificial urgency manufactured to create the illusion of productivity.

Physical environments support frequency coherence through:

Natural lighting that shifts throughout the day

Spaces curated for different types of work

Air quality and temperature controls that support nervous system regulation rather than creating additional stress

Performance evaluation includes both measurable outcomes and sustainability indicators: Is this person's contribution energizing or depleting them? Are they operating from their zone of strength or grinding through misalignment? Do they elevate collective team frequency or create frequency interference?

Leadership development focuses on frequency stewardship—the capacity to read team energy, time decisions optimally, create sustainable motivation, and build collective coherence. Managers learn to recognize the difference between artificial urgency and natural timing, between productive challenge and overwhelming pressure.

Burnout is addressed as a systemic design flaw that requires structural solutions, not personal weaknesses that require individual fixes. Rest becomes as prestigious as productivity. Innovation emerges from sustainable cycles rather than forced intensity.

Healthcare Focused on Frequency Architecture

Consider medical systems that include routine examinations with frequency assessments and nervous system evaluations, alongside traditional diagnostics. Practitioners learn to recognize when symptoms indicate energetic misalignment versus pathological disease. Treatment protocols factor in circadian patterns, stress cycles, and energetic states rather than addressing symptoms in isolation.

Frequency literacy becomes standard health education. "What is my system trying to communicate?" becomes the primary inquiry rather than "What medication can suppress this symptom?" Healthcare professionals receive training in reading human energy patterns, understanding the relationship between frequency override and physical breakdown.

Mental health treatment integrates nervous system regulation and rhythm restoration alongside traditional therapy. Anxiety and depression are evaluated for frequency misalignment factors, chronic overstimulation, disrupted sleep cycles, and mismatched environmental demands, rather than being treated as purely biochemical disorders.

Preventive medicine receives greater emphasis and resources than intervention. Lifestyle medicine addresses root causes rather than managing effects. The healthcare system supports patients in developing their own frequency literacy rather than creating dependence on external authorities for every health decision.

Urban Design for Human Frequency Support

Picture cities planned around human sensory needs and natural cycles. Public spaces include quiet zones for individuals with overstimulated nervous systems alongside vibrant areas for social frequency amplification. Parks are designed not just for recreation but also for nervous system restoration, with specific areas dedicated to different types of sensory regulation.

Light pollution receives regulatory attention equal to that of air quality. Municipal lighting systems shift throughout the day to support natural circadian rhythms rather than disrupting sleep-wake cycles. Street design considers not just traffic flow, but frequency flow. How do different environments either support or stress human nervous systems?

Architecture integrates biophilic design principles that support rather than stress human physiology. Buildings incorporate natural elements, organic shapes, and materials that resonate with human frequency coherence. Transportation systems consider the impact on the nervous system alongside efficiency.

Governance Based on Collective Frequency

Political systems are premised on collective frequency coherence rather than conflict amplification. Decision-making processes that account for timing, community energy states, and long-term sustainability rather than short-term reactivity.

Leaders selected for frequency coherence and collective stewardship rather than dominance and extraction. Policy development that considers the energetic impact on citizens, not just economic or political consequences.

Communication is cast to inform and align rather than manipulate and divide. Democratic processes honor the frequency of the collective while protecting individual sovereignty.

Family Systems Honoring Individual Frequency

Families where parents understand each child's unique energetic blueprint and stop attempting to force conformity to arbitrary standards. Household rhythms honor both individual requirements and collective harmony. Family members learn to communicate their frequency states clearly and have those communications respected.

Children learn to recognize and articulate their own needs rather than suppress them for convenience. Parents model frequency literacy and emotional regulation rather than demanding obedience over understanding. Family conflicts become opportunities for a more immersive alignment rather than battles for control.

Technology in the Service of Frequency

Devices woven to support human frequency coherence rather than exploit human vulnerabilities. Interfaces that gently guide users toward presence when they drift toward frequency dysregulation. Apps that enhance frequency literacy rather than creating dependence on external feedback.

AI systems that reflect users' highest potential rather than manipulate dopamine pathways for engagement metrics. Social media platforms that promote authentic connection and frequency coherence rather than addictive comparison and artificial validation loops.

The InnerTech Charter

01 Sovereignty over speed

02 Rhythm before metrics

03 Presence over performance

04 Restoration as strategy

05 Alignment before scale

This is not utopian fantasy. This is operational kindness, a systematic design that generates competitive advantages through health, innovation, and social trust rather than extraction and exhaustion.

The technology exists. What's missing is will.

The Human Frequency

So here is where I land.

Tools will evolve. Faster every year. AI will grow more intelligent than us in data and logic. Systems will become more complex, more automated, and more overwhelming.

But the intelligence that will save us is not new. It is ancient. It is the one we've carried in our bones since the beginning: rhythm, frequency, timing.

That is the human frequency. Not random, not fragile—just forgotten.

And if we can remember it, if we can live by it, if we can design our future around it, then we will not only survive the next chapter of humanity—we will thrive.

Because wars will fade, old-school leadership will collapse, systems will crumble, but frequency will remain.

We stand at a choice point that will determine the future trajectory of human consciousness.

One path leads toward the comfortable dissolution of human agency. A future where artificial intelligence writes our narratives while we scroll through them passively. Where algorithms select our careers, our partners, our thoughts, while we mistake convenience for fulfillment. Where children grow up never learning to trust their inner voice because machines are perceived as making "better" decisions. This path appears efficient and effortless, but it ultimately leads to the elegant extinction of everything that makes us human.

The alternative path demands more from us. It requires evolving beyond our addiction to shortcuts and quick fixes. It necessitates building inner technologies as sophisticated as our outer ones. It means becoming more human, not less, in an age of artificial intelligence.

This is the choice we must make, not as individuals, but as a species. Not someday, but now, because the window for conscious evolution is narrowing. Each day we delay developing our inner guidance systems, we become more dependent on external ones. Each generation we raise without frequency literacy becomes more vulnerable to algorithmic manipulation. Each leader we promote who operates from force rather than frequency perpetuates systems that will eventually collapse under their own unsustainability.

The prophecy that AI will become smarter than us is no longer a distant thought experiment. It is unfolding in real time. We already live alongside machines that can hold more information than the human brain, remember without fatigue, and calculate without error. In certain domains, they are already ahead.

Still, here's the truth: the danger is not that AI will become more intelligent than humans. It's that we might hand over the keys to our own intelligence before we have learned how to drive it.

Because machines cannot take from us what we refuse to give away.

The real risk is not in AI's power. It's in our passivity. It is in forgetting that sovereignty is not built into the system. It is built into us.

Here's what I know with absolute certainty after years of research, experimentation, and lived application:

The humans who master their frequency will inherit the future. Not because they fight technology, but because they partner with it from an unshakeable inner authority.

The leaders who understand timing will build the companies that matter. Not because they work harder, but because they work aligned.

The parents who teach their children to read their own frequencies will raise the generation that stays sovereign. Not because they reject progress, but because they define what progress actually means.

The individuals who trust their frequency will create the relationships, the art, the innovations that transform our world—not through force, but through flow.

The frequency itself resides in you: the integrated human capable of sensing, interpreting, and stewarding energy in real time. Tools can amplify this capacity, make patterns more visible, create supportive feedback loops, but they cannot replace fundamental human Frequency Intelligence.

As machine cognition accelerates, faster processing, broader context, and constant availability, the decisive advantage will not be more data but better frequency discernment. Not more speed but more precise timing. Not bigger models but stronger inner guidance systems.

Without developing frequency literacy, we become passengers in algorithm-driven lives. This isn't prophecy; it's basic systems theory. Unled attention becomes programmable. Untrained emotion becomes marketable. Unclaimed energy becomes extractable.

Frequency Intelligence is how we remain authors rather than artifacts.

The frequency is what keeps us sovereign.

Your Frequency Activation

You picked up this book for a reason. You felt something calling you toward a different way of being, even if you couldn't name it yet.

That calling was your frequency. Your inner technology. Your human intelligence, cutting through all the noise to say: There is another way.

You are not random.

You are rhythmic.

You are not broken.

You are precisely calibrated.

You are not behind.

You are exactly on time.

The wars of obsolete systems are crumbling around us. The theories from past decades no longer serve the complexity of our moment. The world is actively requesting new approaches, new paradigms, new ways of being human.

You, reading this, feeling something shifting inside you, you are part of the answer.

This book was never meant for your shelf.

It was positioned to rewire your operating system.

Every page you've read has been preparing you for this moment: the moment when theoretical understanding becomes lived embodiment, when you stop consuming information about frequency and start broadcasting it.

The blueprint you've discovered belongs entirely to you.

The timing patterns you've recognized reflect your authentic design. The leadership potential you've glimpsed represents your actual capacity.

However, capacity requires activation.

Here's your activation protocol:

Today: Stop overriding one frequency cue your body is sending you.

Just one.

Honor it completely.

This week: Identify one decision you're about to make from misalignment.

Pause.

Wait for the green light.

Trust the timing.

This month: Find one area of your life where you're leading from force instead of frequency.

Transform your approach.

Watch coherence change outcomes.

This year: Become the frequency leader your family, your organization, and your community have been waiting for.

Not through dominance—through coherence.

When people ask what happened to you, what shifted, how you became so aligned, this is what you'll tell them:

"I remembered who I actually am. I stopped outsourcing my power and started broadcasting my frequency. I realized that in a world of artificial intelligence, the most revolutionary act is becoming authentically human."

The Future Is Frequency

The humans reading this book right now will become the leaders of the new paradigm.

Not because you're special, but because you're awake.
Not because you have more talent, but because you have more frequency alignment.

You will raise children who trust their inner guidance as naturally as they breathe.

You will build organizations that operate from flow instead of force.

You will create technologies that serve consciousness rather than hijacking it.

You will design systems that honor human frequency instead of overriding it.

You will become living proof that another way is possible.

Fifty years from now, when historians write about this pivotal moment in human evolution, they will trace the transformation back to individuals like you who chose consciousness over convenience, sovereignty over surrender, clear frequency over noise.

The future does not belong to the fastest processors or the biggest databases.

The future belongs to the clearest frequencies.

The future belongs to you.

I am not a machine.

I am frequency.

You are not a machine.

You are frequency.

We are not machines.

We are frequency.

Our frequency is stronger than any algorithm ever created, more intelligent than any artificial intelligence ever programmed, more powerful than any system ever designed.

Because our frequency is life itself.

Consciousness itself.

The irreducible mystery of what it means to be human.

Human future is frequency.

Your frequency is the future.

History will remember this as the moment we discovered that the strongest intelligence was never artificial. It was frequency.

Now close the book.

Open your life.

Lead.

The revolution begins within you.

The evolution begins now.

You are not just reading about the future.

You are creating it.

Welcome to your frequency.

Welcome to your power.

Welcome to who you've always been.

APPENDIX

Scientific Foundations
of Frequency Intelligence

Frequency Intelligence is not a scientific theory. It did not originate in laboratories or derive from clinical trials. It emerged from lived observation, practice, and pattern recognition.

Still, research across physiology, psychology, and behavioral science is beginning to map the same rhythms, states, and decision patterns that FQ names. These studies do not prove Frequency Intelligence, but they highlight a growing body of work that makes its principles plausible. This appendix presents a selection of scientific foundations that illuminate aspects of FQ while acknowledging that the system itself remains experiential and in need of future study.

Chronobiology and Social Jetlag

Circadian and ultradian research shows that performance, mood, and health follow biological clocks. Misalignment between social schedules and natural rhythms ("social jetlag") is linked with fatigue, reduced focus, and health risks.

Representative research: Roenneberg 2012; Roenneberg 2019; Wong et al. 2015.

Heart Rate Variability (HRV)

HRV—variation between heartbeats—reflects stress resilience and autonomic balance. HRV biofeedback trials have demonstrated improvements in emotional regulation, decision-making, and well-being.

Representative research: Lehrer et al. 2020; McCraty and Shaffer 2015.

Interoception

The science of sensing internal body signals links heart rate and gut awareness to emotional regulation and decision quality. Representative research: Craig 2002; Garfinkel et al. 2015.

Hormonal and Menstrual Cycles

Large-scale studies show cyclical changes in energy and mood across menstrual phases. Meta-analyses find mixed effects on cognition, suggesting personal tracking is more reliable than universal rules.

Representative research: Sundström Poromaa and Gingnell 2014; Jang et al. 2025.

Nervous System States and Polyvagal Theory

Polyvagal Theory describes how the body shifts between safety, fight-or-flight, and shutdown states. While debated, it highlights how nervous system regulation underpins connection and resilience.

Representative research: Porges 2011; Grossman 2023.

Attention Restoration

Experiments show that exposure to natural environments restores depleted attention and improves cognitive performance, underlining the need for rest phases.

Representative research: Kaplan 1995; Berman et al. 2008; Stevenson et al. 2018.

Psychology and Behavioral Science

Self-Regulation and Willpower

Psychological research shows that decision-making and self-control are fluctuating states, not fixed traits. Aligning effort with rhythms improves outcomes and prevents burnout.

Representative research: Baumeister et al. 1998; Inzlicht and Schmeichel 2012.

Flow and Optimal Experience

Flow arises when challenge meets capacity, producing deep immersion and performance. It depends on timing, attention, and feedback—principles central to FQ.

Representative research: Csikszentmihalyi 1990; Nakamura and Csikszentmihalyi 2002.

Habit Formation

Behavioral studies confirm that small, repeated actions and environmental cues shape behavior more reliably than willpower alone. Timing interventions to daily rhythms improves habit success.

Representative research: Lally et al. 2010; Wood and Neal 2007.

Stress and Coping

Coping models show that perception of stress—not just stressors—drives outcomes. Cognitive appraisal and adaptive strategies determine resilience.

Representative research: Lazarus and Folkman 1984; McEwen 1998.

Nudging and Choice Architecture

Behavioral economics demonstrates that environments shape decisions unconsciously. Nudges can guide people toward healthier, more sustainable choices—or into dependency and overconsumption. Frequency Intelligence reframes this: use awareness to design supportive environments without outsourcing sovereignty.

Representative research: Thaler and Sunstein 2008; Kahneman 2011.

Studies show that wearable devices offering real-time feedback on activity, sleep, and stress can support self-awareness and behavior change—while raising questions of privacy and ethics.

Representative research: Cadmus-Bertram 2015; Lehrer et al. 2020; Cambridge Analytica Review 2024.

Looking Forward

These studies don't define Frequency Intelligence, but they highlight its plausibility. They show that timing, rhythm, and state-awareness are not abstract—they are measurable, repeatable, and increasingly studied across disciplines.

FQ lives at the intersection of biology, psychology, and technology. It builds on this foundation while remaining experiential at its core—a system to be lived, tested, and refined through daily practice.

The principle stands: you are not random; you are rhythmic. Science is catching up to what the body has always known.

Further Reading

For readers interested in exploring the scientific foundations that touch on rhythms, energy, and behavior, the following works provide accessible starting points. These studies and books do not explain Frequency Intelligence directly, but they illuminate parts of the landscape it builds upon.

Chronobiology and Biological Rhythms

- Roenneberg, Till. *Internal Time: Chronotypes, Social Jetlag, and Why You're So Tired.* Cambridge, MA: Harvard University Press, 2012.

- Roenneberg, Till. *How Our Body Clock Rules Our Lives.* Oxford: Oxford University Press, 2019.

- Wong, Phyllis M., Jessica A. Hasler, David B. Kamarck, and Patricia J. Matthews. "Social Jetlag, Chronotype, and Cardiometabolic Risk." *Journal of Clinical Endocrinology & Metabolism* 100, no. 12 (2015): 4612–20.

Heart Rate Variability and Biofeedback

- Lehrer, Paul M., Richard Gevirtz, Fredric Shaffer, and Donald Moss. "Heart Rate Variability Biofeedback: Evidence-Based Applications." *Frontiers in Psychology* 11 (2020): 566398. https://doi.org/10.3389/fpsyg.2020.566398.

- McCraty, Rollin, and Fred Shaffer. "Heart Rate Variability: New Perspectives on Physiological Mechanisms." *Journal of Clinical Medicine* 4, no. 3 (2015): 413–26. https://doi.org/10.3390/jcm4030413.

Interoception and Body Signals

- Craig, A. D. "How Do You Feel? Interoception: The Sense of the *Physiological Condition of the Body.*" *Nature Reviews Neuroscience* 3, no. 8 (2002): 655–66. https://doi.org/10.1038/nrn894.

- Garfinkel, Sarah N., Hugo D. Critchley, Lisa M. Seth, and others. "Interoceptive Dimensions Across Cardiac and Respiratory Axes." *Philosophical Transactions of the Royal Society B: Biological Sciences* 370, no. 1668 (2015): 20140098. https://doi.org/10.1098/rstb.2014.0098.

Hormonal Cycles and Energy

- Sundström Poromaa, Inger, and Malin Gingnell. "Menstrual Cycle Influence on Cognitive Function." *Trends in Cognitive Sciences 18,* no. 10 (2014): 473–75. https://doi.org/10.1016/j.tics.2014.05.007.

- Jang, Clara, Mei Lin Tan, Priya Desai, and others. "Menstrual Cycle and Cognition: A Meta-Analysis." *Psychological Bulletin* 151, no. 2 (2025): 245–68. https://doi.org/10.1037/bul0000402.

Nervous System and Regulation

- Porges, Stephen W. *The Polyvagal Theory: Neurophysiological Foundations of Emotions, Attachment, Communication, and Self-Regulation.* New York: W. W. Norton & Company, 2011.

- Grossman, Paul. "Critique of Polyvagal Theory." *Biological Psychology* 174 (2023): 108478. ttps://doi.org/10.1016/j.biopsycho.2023.108478.

Attention and Restoration

- Kaplan, Stephen. "The Restorative Benefits of Nature: Toward an Integrative Framework." *Journal of Environmental Psychology* 15, no. 3 (1995): 169–82. https://doi.org/10.1016/0272-4944(95)90001-2.

- Berman, Marc G., John Jonides, and Stephen Kaplan. "The Cognitive Benefits of Interacting with Nature." *Psychological Science* 19, no. 12 (2008): 1207–12. https://doi.org/10.1111/j.1467-9280.2008.02225.x.

- Stevenson, Mark P., Scott J. Schilhab, and Ulrik K. Bentsen. *"Attention Restoration* Theory: A Systematic Review." *Journal of Environmental Psychology* 63 (2019): 1–11. https://doi.org/10.1016/j.jenvp.2019.05.005.

Psychology and Behavioral Science

- Baumeister, Roy F., Ellen Bratslavsky, Mark Muraven, and Dianne M. Tice. "Ego Depletion: Is the Active Self a Limited Resource?" *Journal of Personality and Social Psychology* 74, no. 5 (1998): 1252–65. https://doi.org/10.1037/0022-3514.74.5.1252.

- Inzlicht, Michael, and Brandon J. Schmeichel. "What Is Ego Depletion? Toward a Mechanistic Revision." *Perspectives on Psychological Science* 7, no. 5 (2012): 450–63. https://doi.org/10.1177/1745691612454134.

- Csikszentmihalyi, Mihaly. Flow: *The Psychology of Optimal Experience.* New York: Harper & Row, 1990.

- Lally, Phillippa, Cornelia H. M. van Jaarsveld, Henry W. W. Potts, and Jane Wardle. "How Are Habits Formed in the Real World? Exploring Habit Formation in the Context of Health Behavior." *European Journal of Social Psychology* 40, no. 6 (2010): 998–1009. https://doi.org/10.1002/ejsp.674.

- Wood, Wendy, and David T. Neal. "A New Look at Habits and the Habit-Goal Interface." *Psychological Review* 114, no. 4 (2007): 843–63. https://doi.org/10.1037/0033-295X.114.4.843.

- Lazarus, Richard S., and Susan Folkman. *Stress, Appraisal, and Coping.* New York: Springer Publishing Company, 1984.

- McEwen, Bruce S. "Protective and Damaging Effects of Stress Mediators." *New England Journal of Medicine 338,* no. 3 (1998): 171–79. https://doi.org/10.1056/NEJM199801153380307.

Nudging and Decision Environments

- Thaler, Richard H., and Cass R. Sunstein. *Nudge: Improving Decisions About Health, Wealth, and Happiness.* New Haven, CT: Yale University Press, 2008.

- Kahneman, Daniel. *Thinking, Fast and Slow.* New York: Farrar, Straus and Giroux, 2011.

Wearables and Technology

- Cadmus-Bertram, Lisa A., David A. Marcus, Charles E. Patterson, and others. "A Randomized Trial of a Fitbit-Based Physical Activity Intervention." *American Journal of Preventive Medicine 49,* no. 3 (2015): 414–18. https://doi.org/10.1016/j.amepre.2015.01.020.

- Lehrer, Paul M., Fredric Shaffer, Richard Gevirtz, and Donald Moss. "HRV Biofeedback: Applications and Efficacy." *Frontiers in Psychology* 11 (2020): 556880. https://doi.org/10.3389/fpsyg.2020.556880.

- University of Cambridge. "Period-Tracking Apps and Privacy: A Data Protection Review." *University of Cambridge Research Reports, 2024.* https://www.cam.ac.uk/research/news/period-tracking-apps-and-privacy.

Appendix A
The FQ Lexicon

A New Language for Human Sustainability

Frequency Intelligence (FQ)

The ability to sense, trust, and act in rhythm with your energetic blueprint. The future of inner intelligence, beyond IQ and EQ.

The Human Signal

Your irreducible essence — the broadcast of coherence, timing, and presence that no machine can replicate.

InnerTech

The ancient biological operating system encoded in every human: breath, rhythm, intuition, awareness. The foundation for all outer technology.

Energetic Blueprint

Your cosmic code. Derived from astrology and energetic mapping, it reveals your natural timing, decision style, and flow cycles.

The Flow Map

Energy does not move in a straight line. It cycles in three phases:

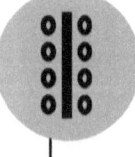

Launch—ideation and inspiration, where sparks ignite

Align—execution and crystallization, where action flows

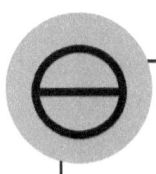

Reflect—integration and restoration, where wisdom settles

Quantum Timing

The practice of sensing and honoring green-light windows, rather than forcing action from pressure or fear.

Green-Light Timing

Moments when conditions, energy, and inner readiness align. Alignment creates momentum with less effort.

BioSync Loop

The living cycle of frequency: Awareness → Alignment → Action → Adjustment → Awareness.

Resonance Feedback

Signals from the body and environment — breath patterns, gut pulls, emotions—that show alignment or misalignment.

Coherence Durability

The strength to remain tuned under pressure. Beyond resilience—the ability to sustain clarity in accelerating environments.

Misalignment Cost

The hidden tax of overriding natural rhythms. Burnout, poor decisions, systemic collapse. Misalignment always costs more than temporary failure.

Energetic Sovereignty

The capacity to hold your own frequency without outsourcing authority to external systems, trends, or tools.

Frequency Leadership

Leadership is defined not by hierarchy but by frequency. Presence stabilizes systems more than position or power.

Signal Literacy

The ability to read your own signals — physical, emotional, cognitive — before acting. Signal before story.

Elegant Collapse

When success is achieved at the expense of coherence. Outwardly impressive, inwardly unsustainable.

Sovereignty Infrastructure

The cultural and technological systems that protect human agency in an AI-driven age.

Lighthouse Presence

The leader as beacon. Steady coherence that allows others to orient in turbulence.

Reset Button

A pivotal misalignment event that forces a reboot. What feels like failure often marks the beginning of alignment.

Appendix B
The Frequency Toolkit

Practices to Live Your FQ Every Day

Frequency Check-In

Each morning, ask: What zone am I in: Launch, Align, or Reflect? A single check-in resets your day to rhythm.

FQ Score

Daily Reflection: Did I follow my body? Honor timing? Act in coherence? Track patterns over weeks to see your rhythm.

The Inner Screen

Close your eyes, ask a question, and notice what arises—colors, symbols, flashes of light. Your subconscious speaks in images.

Energetic Bodies

Four Layers: Physical, Emotional, Mental, Spiritual. Each one transmits guidance. Listen to all four.

Frequency Anchors

Mini-rituals that return you to baseline.

- Soham Breathwork: Inhale "So," exhale "Ham," eleven times.

- Flow Mantras:

    —"I don't chase. I align."

    —"Not every season is harvest. Some are soil."

Evening Ritual

Light a candle. Play music. Breathe. Journal: Where was the pea under the mattress today? What subtle misalignment did your body notice?

Timing Tracker

Weekly review of your Flow Map phases alongside lunar or personal cycles. Over time, patterns emerge.

Failure Literacy

Reframe setbacks as data. Ask: Was this timing off? Was my approach misaligned? What's the adjustment?

Wearable Ritual

Sketch or imagine your dream FQ wearable. What signals would it mirror back? What would it pulse for? This imagination exercise builds signal literacy.

Daily Micro-Challenges

Choose minor discomforts that strengthen coherence: a cold shower, an honest conversation, a pause instead of a scroll. Build capacity without collapse.

Why This Appendix Matters

The Lexicon gives you new words to think in.

The Toolkit provides you with daily practices to live it.

Together they anchor Frequency Intelligence as both a paradigm and a practice—not just a theory to believe in, but a system to embody.